# EVERYWHERE
# IS JERUSALEM

# Everywhere Is Jerusalem: Experiencing the Holy *Then* and *Now*

*Everywhere Is Jerusalem*
978-1-7910-3132-9
978-1-7910-3134-3  eBook

*Everywhere Is Jerusalem: Leader Guide*
978-1-7910-3133-6
978-1-7910-3135-0  eBook

*Everywhere Is Jerusalem: DVD*
978-1-7910-3136-7

James C. Howell

# EVERYWHERE IS JERUSALEM

Experiencing the Holy *Then* and *Now*

Abingdon Press | Nashville

**Everywhere Is Jerusalem**
Experiencing the Holy Then and Now

Copyright © 2024 Abingdon Press
All rights reserved.

**Library of Congress Control Number: 2023947887**
978-1-7910-3132-9

MANUFACTURED IN THE UNITED STATES OF AMERICA

# CONTENTS

*For Hillel Kessler, Connie Beach,*
*and Richard Harrison,*
*who in wonderfully divergent ways*
*have enriched my travels*
*to significant places.*

# INTRODUCTION

## Everywhere Is the Holy Land

All my life I've been itching to go someplace, and after I go I'm compelled to tell about it. I also love to take people along; I take immense pleasure in showing people places that matter to me and to the church and world. I'm even full of recommendations of sights to see and restaurants to frequent if you're heading somewhere I've been. This book is the overflow from the many hundreds of people I've led on dozens of pilgrimages, and seen their minds blown.

With regard to our questions about God, I love to remind folks that we don't have a batch of ethereal, metaphysical truths that float about in the stratosphere of the mind. Everything we believe, the answers to our wonderings, have some real address on planet Earth. And where things happen matters, providing a rich, real world, a real-life context.

Location matters. Jesus wasn't born in some intangible spirituality of heaven, or on a small island in the Pacific, but at the crossroads of the continents. Jesus called his disciples, not in some ivory tower of a university, but when they were busy at work by the edge of a little lake.

St. Francis became St. Francis, instead of just Francis, because he heard God's call, not in the wealthy, safe confines of the walled city of Assisi, but outside the walls, down a steep hill, in a broken-down place in the vicinity of the leper colony everybody else avoided.

# Come on a Journey with Me

I can talk Bible with you in a classroom in a church building (or now online!) all day—and it's great fun. But when people trust me enough to go to Israel, to the shore of Galilee, to the wilderness where Jesus was tested, to Caesarea where Paul was imprisoned, to that broken-down place in Assisi where Francis heard God's call, or closer to my home, across the bridge where John Lewis was nearly beaten to death, or where Martin Luther King Jr. couldn't sleep one night, something magical, transformative, mind-boggling happens.

And when we go, we join a holy throng of pilgrims over the centuries who saved for years, then left family and their livelihoods, enduring hardship and facing intense peril to walk, physically, into sacred places, from Jerusalem to Rome, from Santiago de Compostela at the end of the fabled Camino to the healing waters of Lourdes in France, from Canterbury to Iona. When they got home, I doubt any said, *Check, done that*. For the rest of their lives, they interacted very differently with their family and friends, their chores, the weather, and the lanes of their villages. Jerusalem was, forever in them, everywhere.

I try to picture the homecoming for those pilgrims centuries ago. The elderly, the infirm, the destitute must have rejoiced on their arrival, and then sat spellbound, hanging on every word from the pilgrims who surely realized they had seen everything twice: once for themselves and once for the beloved back home.

For we can't all make such journeys, and for so many reasons. So let me in these chapters take you to some places that are sacred, unforgettable, life-changing. It's not tourism or sightseeing. It's thinking ourselves into a real place where the rest of the world changed—and it might just touch us, virtually, at a distance. In this book, if you'll trust me, I'll take you on a spiritual pilgrimage to significant places in the ongoing story of the Christian faith. We'll go from Bethlehem to Jerusalem, from the Jordan River to Assisi, from the Sea of Galilee to Montgomery, Alabama. Along the way, you'll discover the profound connections between the biblical stories and the places where they happened. You'll see how Christians throughout history have brought their faith to life across the world, in their own cities and communities. And you'll find God calling you to bring your own faith to life right where you are, right now.

> *To grow in faith and holiness, for you to hear God's call and fulfill God's will, you simply must get up and out of the familiar comforts of your home or even your church and go, not to a posh resort or a fun park, but to sacred places where God burst unexpectedly and boldly on the scene and nothing was ever the same.*

I even harbor a firm belief that for you to grow in faith and holiness, for you to hear God's call and fulfill God's will, you simply must get up and out of the familiar comforts of your home or even your church and go, not to a posh resort or a fun park, but to sacred places where God burst unexpectedly and boldly on the scene and nothing was ever the same. Maybe due to personal circumstances you can't go; but you can make the armchair journey with me and see if God materializes for you in imaginative ways.

So this book is part travelogue, but also part Bible study, with meanderings through the history of amazing things God has been doing with amazing people in varied locations. My dream is that, through it all, you will discover that the most important place of all is the place where you are, right now—or that the holy happenings in sacred places might just happen where you happen to be. My journeys can become your journey, to sacred places in your mind and heart, and most importantly, into the mind and heart of God, and thus into the wounds and dreams of God's world.

# Everywhere Is . . . Bethlehem

We begin where Christianity began: in Bethlehem, which reappears in church Christmas pageants and in the mangers in your front yard. But do you know when history's first manger scene actually happened? It took Christianity more than one thousand, two hundred years to witness its first manger scene. And it was none other than the holy, joyful St. Francis of Assisi who figured out how to make Bethlehem real everywhere.

Why was Jesus born in Bethlehem? It was the hometown of Jesus's famous ancestor, Israel's first great king, David. It's just out in the country from the big capital city of Jerusalem—sort of God's typical joke on powerful insiders, using the diminutive, unlikely outsiders. The village's name means "house of bread," which is so fitting. Bethlehem is situated at the crossroads of the continents. Small, accessible, believable. A little town, maybe like one you know.

Driving into Bethlehem today is harrowing. Instead of cruising under strung colored lights and past pretty decorated trees, you cower a bit under heavily armed guard towers, through checkpoints with rifle-toting soldiers. A tall, thick wall dressed with barbed wire reveals intense human fears and our inability to make and keep peace. There are slum-like refugee camps, fitting somehow for the birthplace of Jesus, whose family was immediately on the run, but grievous just the same. Souvenir shops and street hawkers, haggling over little wooden holy trinkets, underline how we delight in making profound religious truths cute and manageable.

Into such a place, plagued by wars, with various invaders jockeying for territory, Jesus came. I love Madeleine L'Engle's thought that when Jesus came, that was

> no time [or place!] for a child to be born,
> With the earth betrayed by war and hate . . . [1]

Far from sweet, God's answer to the crushing powers, to the fear and armed guards, and all the kitsch is a small, vulnerable child who can't talk. He can only cry and coo. He can't be feared or co-opted. He can only be loved and embraced tenderly.

Francis of Assisi intuited all this before anyone else. He asked a friend in the village of Greccio to create history's first manger scene: a straw crib, oxen, donkeys, and an image of the infant Jesus. The townspeople gathered on Christmas Eve, bearing torches. The friars sang hymns, medieval carols, and Francis preached. Listeners said his voice sounded like the bleating of a lamb.

He picked up the infant figure, held it in his arms, and some said they thought they saw the child come to life. Francis's first biographer captured the moment in an elegant phrase: "Out of Greccio is made a new Bethlehem."[2] Before we exhale a sentimental sigh, notice the political weight of the manger scene: Crusaders were at that very moment campaigning to crush those who occupied the Holy Land; they wanted to control Bethlehem militarily. But since Bethlehem now can be anywhere, even in Italy, then there is no longer any need to travel to the Holy Land to fight for it.

# We Are Mothers of God

And so all our manger scenes, in your den or front yard, make the original *"O Little Town of Bethlehem"* virtually present. Perfect love casts out fear—and any desire to control anybody else. At Greccio today, there is perhaps the world's greatest collection of Nativity sets and manger scenes, from every culture, all over the world. Some are gorgeous. Some are laughably tacky. Aren't we always both? Where is the manger right now? Since it was originally a stone feeding trough that served as Jesus's crib, any place where people hunger for hope, love, and purpose: there's the manger. And what are the swaddling clothes right now? The Bible (as Martin Luther loved to say) and all glimpses and signs of God's presence among us.

And who is Mary right now? Not just the one who trudged wearily into Bethlehem to labor in a cow stall, and not all the Marys of paintings, sculptures, anthems, and stained glass. Mary? That would be me, and you, and our church, right now, as the fourteenth-century mystic Meister Eckhart explained:

> "We are all meant to be mothers of God. What good is it to me if this eternal birth of the divine Son takes place unceasingly but does not take place within myself? And what good is it to me if Mary is full of grace if I am not also full of grace? What good is it to me for the Creator to give birth to his Son if I also do not give birth to him in my time and my culture? This, then, is the fullness of time. When the Son of God is begotten in us."[3]

And in Bethlehem. And Greccio. And wherever you are reading this. And in all the broken, crushing places too.

Bethlehem is in the Middle East, as it was when Jesus was born there—but Bethlehem can be anywhere. And we are all asked, like Mary, to make our own journey to Bethlehem and there to bear and birth the reality of God. And so in this book we will look at water and baptism, God's call, courage and taking a stand, prayer and finding home, and finally our death and resurrection, in light of what happened in those locations, locations, locations, and how we find our way to God in the location in which we find ourselves right now.

# CHAPTER 1

# Everywhere Is Galilee

## *The Downward Call*

When I take groups to Israel, we often arrive after dark, which gives them the giddy delight of waking the next morning to sunrise over the Sea of Galilee. How could any sight be more beautiful?

A signature moment comes later that day when we walk out onto the pier at Kibbutz Ginosar and board a large wooden boat, a bit creaky but solid enough, and venture out onto the Sea of Galilee. It's out and back, so we're not going anywhere. It's a spiritual excursion. The waves rock the boat—usually gently, although occasionally, just as we read in the Bible, a squall storms in quickly. My pilgrims scurry for cover, and I get to remind them that this is the real Bible experience.

You catch glimpses of the little villages on the shoreline where most of the Gospels happened, with mountains looming like guardians behind them. When we get to roughly the middle of the eight-mile-wide sea, the captain asks me "Now?" and turns off the engine. After a short reading about Jesus stilling the storm (Mark 4), and "Be still, and know that I am God" (Psalm 46:10), we simply rest together on the water. The boat bobs a little, the waves rhythmically brushing the sides of the boat; a gentle breeze courses through. Too soon the reverie ends as the motor roars into gear to take us back to shore. Beautiful. Moving.

Usually. Riskier than the sudden arrival of a storm is the chance of the silence being shattered by another boatload of believers nearby—who seem to believe the Psalm says "Make noise and know that I am God," with pop Christian music blaring on the loudspeaker. Nothing ruins our relationship with God quite like other believers, right?

And then, while I never bring up the subject while we're floating on Galilee, I worry about the ways a spiritual excursion, either our quiet, pensive experience, or the higher volume singing of the other guys, can serve as a shiny, emotional substitute for what happened with the original disciples in their boats on that same sea. It was hardly a spiritual rush for them. They found themselves asking, as we hesitate to ask, not *What do I want to do?* or even *What do I want to do for God?* but *What does God want me to do?* For them, nothing was ever the same. Changed livelihoods, their families puzzled and upset, risking their futures and very lives because of an encounter on Galilee.

# The Jesus Boat

After we disembark, I lead my friends into a lovely little museum that houses what we call the "Jesus boat." In 1986, when the water level hit record lows due to drought, two fishermen (who fancied themselves as amateur archaeologists) bumped into something that turned out to be perhaps the greatest archaeological find ever in that region: a twenty-seven-foot-long fishing boat from the time of Jesus. Extricating it from the mud (which had preserved it for two millennia!) required engineering that was daring and sheer genius, verging on the miraculous. I find myself wishing that something like *S.S. Simon Peter* or *Zebedee & Sons Inc.* had been carved on its prow.

That boat is a palpable reminder of the earthy reality of the Bible's stories. Did Jesus step into this boat? Maybe. He saw it, for sure, and most likely interacted with its owners who sailed it, patched its leaks (the wood shows us where!), and earned their living in that open-air wooden office we can almost reach out and touch today. Christianity isn't some vague, invisible spirituality within. Jesus stepped into the waves, mud, corded nets, and smelly fish of real life. Those first disciples, who never dreamed they'd be remembered as anything so hifalutin, knew nothing of what we rank as a spiritual experience. The biggest miracle by the sea wasn't the stilling of the storm or the miraculous catch of fish. It was that these laborers, at their work, with dependent families at home, met a guy and simply dropped everything and traipsed off after him.

I'd have asked some hard questions. Follow me? Where? For how long? How will it all work out? What's the strategy? But with reckless foolhardiness, they just left it all and followed him... to who knows where. Abraham had done the same. The Lord told him, "Go from your country...to the land that I will show you" (Genesis 12:1). Awfully open-ended, wasn't it?

There must have been some beauty about Jesus. Something utterly compelling. I try to ponder this while floating on Galilee, standing on the shoreline, and gazing at that ancient boat. Not What can I *feel* in this place about Jesus? but *What is Jesus asking of me, with my real life?* Jesus came to the grimy, sweaty workplace of real people. A Jesus place. Not a pretty church sanctuary, but out in the busy, hardscrabble world where nobody was being very pious. And that is where our journey with him begins and happens.

# Down, Down, Down

Can Galilee be anywhere, everywhere? Can I find myself on the shore of that sea? Lucky me: my call story involves a dream in which Jesus (how did I recognize him?) spoke two words to me by the Sea of Galilee: "Follow me." A reluctant, cynical, and relatively new churchgoer, I woke up and asked my roommate when that Bible study he'd been nagging me to try met next. Tonight? I went, guardedly, but with the vividness of my dream rattling in my head. After snacks and chitchat, the leader opened his Bible and said, "Let's look at Matthew 4 where Jesus says 'Follow me.'"

What is God's call? What's my journey now? Perhaps instead of asking How can we hear God's call? we should ask *Where* can we hear God's call? Call happens in a place. Any place is possible, but my travels have persuaded me you're way more likely to hear God's call in certain kinds of places, maybe daunting places you might normally avoid, while the comfortable places might desensitize our call antennae.

Let's go back to Assisi, and where St. Francis heard God's call. Yes, he stood between the candles in the cathedral and asked the priest to open the Bible at random. Wherever his fingers and eyes landed, that would be God's call for Francis. Gutsy, this faith as "willingness for whatever" (Maggie Ross's phrase),[1] but rash, way too risky. You might land on "Sell all you have and give it to the poor."

Which is precisely what happened to Francis! And he responded: Got it. Done. But his quest to discern God's will was more complex and took a long time. Feeling restless and unfulfilled, although he was wealthy, hip, and popular, he began to walk every day out from the city walls of Assisi down a sharp hill to a little crumbling church, San Damiano. He went down, down, down, to a shabby, broken-down place where the poorest of the poor lived. If we're serious about hearing God's call, we leave our secure place, and go down—like Jesus did, like Francis did. We find a way to an uncomfortable place and to people and situations the world might deem lowly.

In that low place, Francis prayed, not "Lord, make me an instrument of your peace," but this: "Most high, glorious God, enlighten the darkness of my heart and give me, Lord, correct faith, firm hope, perfect charity, wisdom and perception, that I may do what is truly your most holy will."[2] Humble, hopeful, and committing himself to *do* whatever. He didn't pray this once and expect a reply. He prayed it repeatedly every day, and for many months. Finally he heard the cross before which he knelt speak to him: "Francis, rebuild my church, for it is falling into ruin."

> *Dietrich Bonhoeffer showed us that God's call isn't about keeping your hands clean, being good, but getting your hands dirty for God. Our journey isn't one of upward mobility, but downward mobility.*

Notice his calling, like all true callings, wasn't for him or even about him. It was outward, other-directed. His task, like ours, was to make the church healthier. He started small, using masonry skills he'd picked up in the military to fix up San Damiano, not yet understanding it was the Church, capital C, not just that little church, God had in mind. His hands got scraped and dusty. Dietrich Bonhoeffer showed us that God's call isn't about keeping your hands clean, being good, but getting your hands dirty for God. Our journey isn't one of upward mobility, but downward mobility.

I have journeyed down that steep hill to San Damiano a dozen times. I always exit feeling inspired—but then I turn to go back to the hotel, the same turn Francis would have made to return home each day. A long, steep hill, a tough climb. Doing God's will is hard. It's an uphill battle. For Francis, at the end of that arduous trek home were his parents, who had very different dreams for their son, good dreams, the kind Americans harbor: more wealth, comfort, success. How often does pursuing what God asks puzzle and even mortify people we love?

His parents, Pica and Pietro, fine, churchgoing, upstanding citizens, found themselves increasingly appalled by their son's reckless behavior. It came to the point they had him arrested and put on trial for squandering family resources in his campaign to be like Jesus and help the poor. Francis solemnly removed all he had left from his earthly family: the clothes on his back. With his eyes fixed upward, he declared, *"From now on I will say* freely: *'Our Father who art in heaven,'* and not 'My father, Pietro di Bernardone.'"[3] For the rest of his days, Pietro would turn away or spit on the ground if he passed his son on the street.

I resonate (with a bit of PTSD) to this story, as my father was similarly mortified by my decision to enter Christian ministry. So many well-meaning parents assume they can pinpoint the best life direction for their children, and thereby can be hazardous to the kids pursuing their journey into God's calling.

When Pope Francis visited Assisi, it was at the square where St. Francis renounced his earthly goods that the Pope said Mass. His vision of how to be Pope wasn't about finery, pomp, and power, but humility, shedding power, empowering the poor, getting his hands dirty, doing what Jesus would do, the things Jesus told all of us to do.

Francis had no idea how it would all turn out. He would have blushed and laughed out loud if we could travel back in time and tell him he'd be such a great saint, that Church changed because of him, or that little statues of him would function as bird feeders in gardens! When God called Abraham, Moses, Ruth, Jeremiah, Peter, Paul, Mary, and those fishermen, God didn't map out a strategy or pledge how swimmingly well it would all go. Jesus said "Follow me," and they dropped their nets, their livelihood and security, and traipsed off after him, clueless of what was next or what the end game would be. Jesus hadn't asked them to be good, to feel more spiritual, or to engage in little spurts of seasonal charity. He'd asked them to have some courage, to make a journey, to stick close to him, not to their cherished ideas of good.

# Sitting Around in Paris

How can you leave what's safe for you, and go down…and pray Francis's prayer, and then make the long hard climb back into the world, but changed? Notice how many light years this is from our modern quests for spiritual experience and, above all else, comfort. If I ask my church people what they want from church, many will answer "Comfort," which I understand. But come with me to Paris. I love Paris, which has earned its status as "romantic" and "beautiful." I've preached there, at the American church. And I've thrilled to the bridges, the lovely streets, the cathedrals, and the Père Lachaise cemetery, where dozens of luminaries are buried; the fact that Chopin is just a few feet from Jim Morrison makes me smile.

But the specter of war and intense suffering always lingers in the shadows. During the Nazi occupation, a nun from Latvia, Maria Skobtsova, found her way to Paris, where she sheltered Jewish children. The Gestapo arrested her, and she perished in a gas chamber at Ravensbrück on Holy Saturday, 1945. Her memory is marked at Yad Vashem outside Jerusalem as one of "the Righteous

Among the Nations." Mother Maria (now St. Maria of Paris) wrote words for us all:

> It would be a great lie to tell searching souls: "Go to church, because there you will find peace." The opposite is true. She tells those who are at peace and asleep: "Go to church, because there you will feel real alarm about your...sins, about the world's sins....There you will find an unappeasable hunger for Christ's truth. There instead of lukewarm you will become ardent, instead of pacified you will become alarmed, instead of learning the wisdom of this world you will become foolish in Christ."[4]

Stay with me in Paris. In the 1950s, the great writer James Baldwin had gone there to escape the racial tension in America. Paris seemed ideal, with so much charm and cultural panache, safely remote from the ugliness devouring America.

But one day he picked up the newspaper and saw photographs from Charlotte, North Carolina—where I live. There she was: Dorothy Counts (a good friend of ours today) when she was fifteen years old, in 1957, walking into Harding High School as the first (and only one that day) to integrate our all-white schools. Menacing white kids surrounded her in the photos, jeering, spitting, and throwing rocks.

Baldwin stared and was shaken:

> There was an unutterable pride, tension, and anguish in that girl's face. It made me furious, it filled me with both anger and pity, and it made me ashamed. Some one of us should have been there with her! I dawdled in Europe for nearly yet another year, held by my private life...but it was on that bright afternoon that I knew...I could, simply, no longer sit around in Paris....Everybody else was paying their dues, and it was time I went home and paid mine.[5]

The call came in the alarming morning news, in a comfortable place, sparking a journey to an uncomfortable place. He came home and entered the fray.

# The Dexter Avenue Parsonage

God's call isn't so much doing nice things for God. And it isn't "taking a stand," which is usually nothing more than passing judgment on somebody. God's call is about standing with the Dot Countses of our world and paying our dues instead of relishing whatever cozy space we've woven around ourselves. Where might your journey involve standing close to someone being marginalized? Some wise person said that if you count yourself an ally of some group of people, but you aren't getting hit by the stones being thrown at them, then you aren't standing close enough.

Do we realize Dr. Martin Luther King Jr. did not move to Montgomery to champion civil rights? He sought a nice church with nice people where he could enjoy a nice pastorate. I've taken folks to visit the Dexter Avenue Baptist Church in Montgomery, and the church parsonage nearby that was firebombed in January 1956, and to places that mattered in his life: his birthplace on Auburn Avenue in Atlanta, and the Ebenezer Baptist Church where his father Mike was pastor, followed by King Jr., adjacent to his tomb at the King Center. I've walked across the Edmund Pettus Bridge in Selma and stood on the steps of the Lincoln Memorial. The Lorraine Motel in Memphis, where he was assassinated, is a moving location, not to mention the Birmingham jail and Boston University where he studied.

Whose life more dramatically embodies the common phrase, *Location, location, location*? When Dr. King greeted parishioners on the front steps at Dexter, the steps of the Alabama State Capitol where Governor Wallace spewed venom were just a stone's throw away on the same street. Had King crossed a bridge in Canada instead of Selma, no one would have noticed. If he'd shared his dream at Disneyland instead of the National Mall in Washington, we'd find it humorous.

Like Jesus and all the great heroes and change agents through history, Dr. King walked directly into the teeth of danger, into places he was certainly not welcome and at risk of bodily harm. A brilliant orator, his words were ridiculed where he spoke them.

When I stand where something courageous and revolutionary happened, I try to feel what's coming up out of the ground into my feet and body. My son Noah and I stood on the porch of the Dexter Avenue parsonage where a firebomb nearly destroyed the house with Mrs. King and their young daughter inside. Our driver, an old quiet gentleman, after we stood there silently for a few minutes, said "I was there that night—when I was about the age of your son." I trembled and asked him all he could recall— when an angry crowd assembled and King stunned them by saying, "Don't get panicky. Don't do anything panicky. Don't get your weapons.... Remember...what Jesus said....We want to love our enemies....Be good to them....What we are doing is right. What we are doing is just. And God is with us."[6]

Lisa and I walked across the Edmund Pettus Bridge. No opposition, no billy clubs, no lashing tongues, but I tried to feel the immense courage, hope, and determination to change the world rising up through my feet, which are so very soft from my life of comfort. Somebody prodded me to pose for a photo in the Dexter pulpit. I did, grinned, and then felt so very small and foolish.

You can read about the Lorraine Motel in a book, or you can watch a documentary. Or you can just go about your life of busyness and diversion and not think about it at all. But if you go to Memphis, then, instead of fixating on barbecue and Elvis, pay a visit to the

Lorraine. There's something holy, or unnerving, about standing on that balcony where he came out to get some fresh air with his friends who'd enjoyed a pillow fight the night before—and then he was gone. Across the street you can see where James Earl Ray fired that fatal shot before he fled, managing to elude authorities for more than two months and into four countries!

> *In our pathetically divided America, some see racism everywhere, and some think it's a thing of the past. Personally, I feel sure God wants me to listen to the people who might be vulnerable or the victims of ongoing, sneaky racism. If I ask, and listen, they can tell me.*

In our pathetically divided America, some see racism everywhere, and some think it's a thing of the past. Personally, I feel sure God wants me to listen to the people who might be vulnerable or the victims of ongoing, sneaky racism. If I ask, and listen, they can tell me. I am sure God would rather me err on the side of suspecting that much work on such deeply ingrained attitudes isn't done yet. And I am sure God asks me, and all of us, to have some courage, to take note that what happened at the King places you can easily visit didn't happen centuries ago. My driver in Montgomery was there. Feels like hard work—and it is, like everything else that's meaningful.

During the Montgomery bus boycott, a taxi driver pulled up beside a much beloved older woman known as Mother Pollard and asked if he could give her a ride. She insisted on walking, saying "My feets is tired, but my soul is rested."[7] I've walked all over her Montgomery, Selma, Birmingham, and Atlanta. I guess my feet get tired. But the walk does rest my soul.

# St. Francis of Lithuania

To hear God's call, we go down, down, down. But you don't have to travel all that far to find the down location where God invites you to engage. Sometimes it's close to home. Jesus, and his friend Francis of Assisi, might just show up in utterly unanticipated places. Like for me in Lithuania.

Years ago, our church got involved in the rekindling of Methodism in Lithuania, as the country was coming to life after years of Communist suppression. We plugged in to the small city of Šiauliai, where I have friends to this day. We got hold of a building that once had been a train station, then a Soviet army recruiting center, and we morphed it into a Methodist church. I love the symbolic, revolutionary power of that.

On the outskirts of Šiauliai is an unforgettable sight, virtually a miracle. A long time ago, people erected a few crosses on a hill as a symbol of Lithuanian independence. When the Russians seized power after World War II, the Communists bulldozed the site. But Lithuanians sneaked onto the hill that night and put up several crosses—which were summarily removed, only for more to appear the next night. Finally the authorities quit bothering. The hill is now marvelously crammed with over 100,000 crosses, large and small, simple and ornate. A sacred, pro-Christian, anti-Communist statement of defiance and hope.

My daughter and I were wandering among the thicket of crosses when she noticed a brick building in the distance. Curious, we strolled down the path until arriving at what turned out to be a Catholic monastery. The monks welcomed us inside, and the circular sanctuary featured a series of stained glass windows narrating the life of St. Francis, in the same way churches in and near Assisi have frescoes depicting the very same scenes. Sarah and I had just come to Lithuania from—you guessed it—Assisi. Our jaws dropped.

Then we met the answer to Henri Nouwen's oft-repeated question: "Who will be the St. Francis of our age?"[8] Her name? Regina Židonienė. Born and raised an atheist, she got involved with a tiny Methodist house church in Birzai, converted to Christianity, and became a whirling dervish working for her church and in mission. You would count her as poor, living in a very small house (where I've slept) with no running water or other comforts. But she expends her time going to the people she thinks of as poor, the poorest of the poor. I've been with her several times to deliver medicine and food to people she's befriended who live in horrid conditions. She creatively finds ways to provide for them. She knows them, loves them, mentors them, admonishes them, and prays for them.

We visited a young woman whose boyfriend Regina told me was "trouble." After we filled the makeshift kitchen with food, I watched her lecture this young woman sternly to avoid this man, and then we prayed. Regina prayed, that is—at length, and in Lithuanian. I felt in the moment it was the single most powerful time of prayer in my life, without understanding a word. God was in our holy circle.

When she was done, I asked her what she'd prayed about. She'd told me she'd called down a curse on this abusive boyfriend, and then blessings for the women's children, by name and in great detail about their lives, for health, faith, hope, nutrition, and employment. I pitied the poor boyfriend. I heard later he oddly never showed his face there again.

Regina and I continue to be friends, talking fairly often, after nearly two decades now. When the war broke out in Ukraine, she organized shelter, food, and medicine for nearly two hundred Ukrainian refugees, who have decided to stay there in Birzai, so great was the community of love they found there. The mayor recently awarded her a lifetime merit plaque for her long and tireless work with and advocacy for the poorest of the poor.

I asked her once, "Regina, why do you do all this work?" She was puzzled I would ask such a thing, and responded, "Why, this is just what Christians do, isn't it?" The voice of St. Francis echoed across the centuries in her words, and I saw a fresh incarnation of him, a simple Christian doing what Christians do, in her hands and feet, her whole body and self.

# Not Jesus's Girlfriend

The God who called all creatures into existence can and does call any and everyone. Who are we to question anybody else's call? Part of my hearing God's call is delighting in the way God calls others, especially the unlikely ones (unlikely, that is, only from our flawed, narrow viewpoint, but never unlikely in God's own heart and mind).

One of the most spectacular excavations in recent years has been on the shore of the Sea of Galilee: the village of Magdala, the home of Mary Magdalene. It's been there for centuries, waiting to be dug up. A synagogue was found, along with an amazing stone decorated with a menorah, apparently a lector's table that held the Torah scroll. Didn't Jesus grasp it as he read and taught in that synagogue?

The enigmatic Mary Magdalene looms large in the story of Jesus. She is named alongside the twelve disciples in Luke 8:2; she, Joanna, and Susanna ("and others") are counted as if they, too, were disciples—and these three women appear to be the ones bankrolling the operation! Joanna is especially intriguing: she's "the wife of Chuza, Herod's steward." Turns out he was the wealthy business manager of the entire province. What scandal was there for him, and what tension in his household, when his wife, instead of entertaining wealthy dignitaries, traipsed off after this poor teacher who was already being hounded by government officials as dangerous?

Mary Magdalene, Luke tells us, "had been healed of evil spirits," including "seven demons." Dirty-minded theologians over the centuries leaped to the conclusion she was a hooker—which says more about their mindset than her reality. In art, she is often depicted as sultry, even after her conversion! And with red hair, an artistic code implying something tawdry. But no Jewish woman of the first century had red hair. If anything, she was a person of substance, positive renown, and respect—at least until she traipsed off after Jesus! Of course, *The DaVinci Code* made her into Jesus's girlfriend, which says more about the tastes of modern audiences than about the real Jesus and Mary.

Jesus didn't exactly ride the crest of the wave of women's empowerment as we know it today. And yet there are shocking clues into his revolutionary ways. Remember the story of the other Mary and her sister Martha? Jesus comes for dinner. Martha fulfills the time-honored female role of whipping up the meal in the kitchen. But her sister Mary defies all convention by sitting at Jesus's feet and soaking up his teaching. Only men were allowed! Martha chides Jesus for allowing this, but he replies, "Mary has chosen the good portion" (Luke 10:38-42). That we know about Mary Magdalene, Joanna, and Susanna is extraordinary. With them, and with some women we read about in Acts, we see the very beginnings of a gender revolution. The world wasn't ready, and in some ways still hasn't quite arrived.

In Assisi, a young woman named Clare lived with her family right next door to the cathedral, San Rufino. She probably watched Francis preach in the square outside the cathedral from her window. Clare was so moved by the radical lifestyle and joyful witness of Francis and his friends that she eluded an arranged marriage, sneaked off from her family on Palm Sunday night, and joined Francis and his friars. Other women flocked to her movement. Mind you, they sequestered the women in their own space, as churchmen back then still fretted about their charms.

The beautiful church the Catholics built at Magdala, the only church in Israel dedicated to women, has the Latin words *Duc in Altum* carved over the entrance: "Cast Out into the Deep," which Jesus said to the disciples in Luke 5 after they'd not caught any fish all night. He's not simply giving fishing instructions. He's urging them to get beyond the surface of things, to go deep, to probe the depths of themselves, others, the world, and God. Magdala reminds us of the ways we've splashed around in the shallow end of the life of faith, not plunging into the depths of the heart of God, and not finding a more profound way to deal with human difference.

> *When God's glory is fully manifest,*
> *we will all of us shine like the sun,*
> *nobody ranked or used by anybody else.*

Of course, the depth we're after isn't political or social, although politics and society will be impacted. It's about the goodness of God shown off in every person, not a flattened-out equality but a sheen of glory that celebrates difference, the way a rainbow isn't just blue or orange but a full spectrum of color. Eventually, when God's glory is fully manifest, we will all of us shine like the sun, nobody ranked or used by anybody else. Like Jesus—oh, and Mary, and Mary, and Clare, and you.

# What Kind of a Christian Are You?

God's call can lead to a big decision, taking the road less travelled, or making a total U-turn from where you'd been heading. God's call also is constant, weekly, daily, hourly. What now? What's next? Naturally, the God-given muscles within that say yes to God's call can get flabby; we hit cruise control and the days slide by. Just because we presume we're well inside God's calling doesn't mean we've not drifted. Getting out of the comfort zone, making a deliberate journey to an unfamiliar place can provide the space we need to hear God's call in some fresh, new way. Usually it involves somebody you didn't know five minutes earlier, that "angel unaware," the guise God puts on to reawaken the call in us.

On a train, rumbling toward the outskirts of London, I had an encounter with such an angel. On the last leg of a long trip through England, my kids were weary. I thought I'd pass the time and keep them awake by quizzing them: "How did the Gettysburg address begin?" "Who comprised the Second Triumvirate?" "Can you count to ten in Spanish?" A groan or two, but they tried.

When I asked, "Can you name the books of the Bible?" another train-rider across the aisle turned, and his eyes zoomed in on us. I'd noticed him earlier, sitting there with a little boy. He seemed to want to chat, but I avoided eye contact. He watched attentively as my son began, "Genesis, Exodus..." and when there was a pause before "1 Chronicles," the man interrupted (to my children's relief) by asking (in a charming cockney accent) "Are you a Christian, man?"

I couldn't wriggle out now, so I replied, "Yes," which led him to ask, "What *kind* of a Christian are you?" How to answer? I kept it simple: "Methodist." "Methodist?" He shook his head, as if I had just told him I suffer from some chronic disease. "Where I come from, Methodists don't take their faith seriously, they just go through the motions, it has no real impact on their lives, it's just a social thing." I assured him, "Oh, we don't have that problem where *I* come from." My oldest rolled her eyes.

Then he explained to me that he was a gypsy. Not sure I'd ever interacted with a gypsy. Then he launched into a lengthy description of the gypsy church, how even though other churches across Europe barely register a pulse, the gypsy church is booming, growing, vital, even if unnoticed. In Hungary, Spain, France, Italy, and England, gypsies are being converted and are joining thriving bodies of believers.

My new friend Caleb went on to explain that it's not easy for gypsies to become disciples of Jesus. "Do you know what the most common and best paid profession is for gypsies?" I shrugged. "Fortune-teller. When you become a Christian, you can't be a fortune-teller anymore. So people have to give up their livelihood, and support of their families. We're asking a lot."

I asked if they couldn't just pretend, since fortune-telling isn't real anyhow. But no, fortune-telling dabbles in the occult, and claims for itself what is not true; to be the kind of a Christian God wants, you have to give it up. I pondered for a few moments what professions American Christians would never forsake, all the careers of fortune-making about which the Church seems to have no opinion. The gypsy church is "asking a lot," and it is booming. In America, we ask for next to nothing.

I'd noticed Caleb's young son with a book with the English alphabet, and some simple, basic reading sentences. I assumed the boy was learning to read. But no. It was Caleb learning to read: "Gypsies don't go to school, and gypsies don't read. But I am training to be a minister—like you!—and so I have to learn to read. It's hard...but I can't wait until I can read God's Word—like you!" I sorted through in my mind the novels, biographies, and tour books stashed away in my carry on bag...and then, at about that moment, the train slowed to a halt at the station. We gathered our bags and lingered on the platform with our new friends to say goodbye. Caleb had one last question: "What are you doing tonight? We have a service at half-seven, lots of gypsies coming. We would love for you to come." I looked at my wife and remembered our family's grand plan to grab a bite and then watch the movie, *Scooby-Doo*.

I think in that moment I perceived all that was wrong with the Church, and in me. I'd just met the hope of the Church: a gypsy who, like the Son of Man, had no place to lay his head. His name, after all, was Caleb, namesake of Joshua's friend who scouted out enemy territory and believed God would deliver. This Caleb lured us away from the movie house into a raucous service of humble prayer and holy praise with some ex-fortune-tellers, with his lingering, perfectly targeted question, "What kind of a Christian are you?"

# Living with Moses

How can I stick closer to the kind of Christian God asks me to be? Could I commit to a sustained lifetime of reading, pondering, reflecting, praying, conversing, going down, far from the place of comfort? It's a radical reconstruction of the will—which isn't my freedom to do as I wish, but my being liberated to be bound tightly and irrevocably to God, sticking very close to Jesus. Come with me again to Rome, and let's visit three sites many tourists miss.

If you walk from the Roman Forum past the Colosseum, turn left, and climb the Esquiline Hill, past several lovely trattorias and flower shops, you'll arrive at San Pietro in Vincoli: St. Peter in Chains, so named because the relics under the altar, behind glass, are supposedly the chains that bound Peter when he was imprisoned in Rome. Don't they invite me to ponder my own bonds of obedience to God's will? "Let thy goodness, like a fetter, bind my wandering heart to thee."[9]

Peter wasn't chained for political activism or criminal activity. In John 21, Peter affirms his love for Christ, but then learns that he'll be bound by such love to go to difficult places and tasks. Peter was called to Rome, where he was bound in fetters and eventually executed. We are asked, not to seek comfort from God, but to go and do what God asks, no matter the cost.

But nobody pays much attention to the chains in St. Peter in Chains because just to the right of that altar is Michelangelo's striking sculpture of Moses. It's massive: he's eight feet tall—seated! There's so much energy captured in his face, hands, and posture; his foot looks poised to spring up. His piercing gaze is a bit intimidating, but wise, visionary.

Pope Julius hired Michelangelo to build his tomb, with Moses, but it took him more than three decades to finish it, always perfecting it, and distracted by other work (like the Sistine Chapel!). He chipped away at the marble in his workshop near St. Peter's— which was his home, where he lived. Art historian William Wallace explains that "Michelangelo lived with Moses; the two grew old together. Every morning the artist woke up with Moses. Every time he returned home, he was welcomed by the same imposing figure. To live with Moses could be unnerving."[10]

I wonder what it would be for you and me to "live with Moses," and to "grow old together." Moses: a man of immense courage and resilience, a dogged determination to do God's will in the face of peril and frustration. Moses: the custodian of God's law, showing us how to live with God and others. Moses: the mystic, withdrawing from the crowd to be alone with God on a mountain. I am pondering spending more time with Moses as I grow older, his life and experiences, and the words he shared, so challenging, and so hopeful. Jesus pondered Moses every day. All of Scripture, Moses and the rest, might just sustain in me a keen attentiveness to God's ongoing call. Even the grisly sacrifices of Exodus, Leviticus, and Numbers: being chained to Jesus requires sacrifice. It's not doing enjoyable, rewarding things for God, but what is hard, as we bear the cost to discipleship.

Wallace humorously envisions the day they moved that massive statue three miles from Michelangelo's home to *San Pietro in Vincoli*: "A few astonished persons stood gaping as Moses, peering over the side of a rude cart, slowly rolled through the streets of Rome."[11] Moses, watching us on the street: oh my.

# My Aching Knees

A couple of miles southeast of Moses is the massive San Giovanni in Laeterno. When St. Francis visited Rome for his first time, he knocked on the door of this, the papal residence and grandest of all churches in Rome. The doorkeeper informed the pope that a poor man, shabbily dressed, was there to see him. The pope said to send him away.

But that night the pope had a vivid, disturbing dream: the magnificent building was falling down, but it was being propped up by a poor, shabbily dressed man. He sent the doorkeeper to find the poor man. Francis returned and submitted his plan for his new Order of Friars. His strategy was laughable, really just a string of Bible verses about things Jesus did. His draft for a new Catholic order was simply *We want to do the things Jesus did*.

St. Dominic also visited. Brimming with pride, the pope directed his attention to the glorious architecture and exquisite ornamentation in bronze, ivory, and precious metals, and declared, "No longer can it be said, 'Silver and gold have I none'"—a clever allusion to what Peter said to the beggar in Acts 3:6. Dominic wryly responded, "Yes, but also you can no longer say 'In the name of Jesus, rise up and walk!'"—which is what Peter did for the man in Acts 3!

Across the busy street from San Giovanni is the *Scala Sancta*, a long staircase, allegedly the very twenty-eight white marble steps from Pontius Pilate's palace in Jerusalem that Jesus descended after being condemned to death. Helen, the mother of the emperor Constantine, had them hauled all the way to Rome!—if you believe such things. For centuries, pious pilgrims have climbed those steps on their knees.

I have awful knees, but decided it was now or never to join Francis, Dominic, Martin Luther, and tens of thousands of pilgrims holier than I'll ever be. Tempted many times over that long hour to quit, I made it to the top. My knees ached for days, a palpable reminder of a physical devotion to something deeply spiritual, even if a little bit crazy.

Do I seek just comfort from God? Does God want me to be as comfortable as possible? Could it be that God might lure me into something uncomfortable? If I deliberately take on something arduous and even painful for God, something I could easily avoid, might this actually build some spiritual strength in me? Francis slept and knelt on solid rock, for crying out loud.

And so this itinerary to Galilee, with its waves lapping up all the way to Italy, Montgomery, and even Lithuania: Can the call find its way to me where I am right now? And continue to echo, so I can answer yes again and again? Where can I go down to hear more clearly? Can I live with Moses, and Francis, and even dare to be like Francis of Lithuania? Could I be the Francis of... my place? That would require considerable recklessness and courage, wouldn't it? Think you're too old? You're not as old as Abraham yet. Bedridden? God still calls. Can't bust loose from your commitments? Start small—and you might wind up like Francis.

# CHAPTER 2

# Everywhere Is the Jordan

## *Baptism and All the Waters*

When I take groups to the Holy Land, people are shocked by how narrow and shallow the Jordan River is. More of a creek! And muddy. Even allowing for changing levels over the centuries, it's still so modest.

We drive a hot, dusty road from Jericho to Qasr al-Yahud, which scholars believe is very close to (if not the very spot) where John baptized Jesus. Just a few feet wide, brownish, Israel on this bank, the country of Jordan on the other. You could tiptoe twenty feet across and touch off an international incident. Once when we were there, a Korean pilgrimage group on the other side sang "How Great Thou Art" in their language. Moved, we echoed it back to them in English. I sensed God's worldwide Church was asking, "Shall We Gather at the River?" Yes, we did that day. And how great art Thou? So very great.

The Jordan, so narrow, so shallow, and with so much history, deep with biblical resonance, draws pilgrims in, almost compelling them to pull off their shoes and wade in. No one says anything. Hard to believe, but they almost forget to snap selfies. I try to decipher their tears, bowed heads, and joyful smiles. I wonder if the smallness is the allure. It's so humble, so accessible. A wide swath of roaring rapids would terrify, not welcome. God's river says, *Come, any, all of you.*

Jesus waded into that same shallow stream—to be baptized by John, but probably other times as well. Can we see him bathing off the dust of the wilderness on another visit? Did he ever fish in that river with his friends? At the baptism, what were his inner thoughts? I doubt he merely thought, "Wow, what a cool spiritual experience!" He was always wise. He saw further and deeper than we do, his perspective never whittled down to just the here and now or what was obvious to others. Did he contemplate Israel crossing over to the Promised Land a millennium earlier, or Elijah and that chariot of fire nearby? Did he ponder the flow of that water, and the contours of the banks and hills the river had carved out over many millennia?

# And A River Runs Through It

Has Jesus inspired other writers since then, unbeknownst even to themselves, regarding water? As my wife, Lisa, and I finished up our vacation in Yellowstone National Park, we took the West Yellowstone exit and turned north toward Bozeman. I slowed and then stopped when I noticed, on my left, a sparkling stream where two men were fly-fishing. Wasn't *A River Runs Through It* filmed here? I surprised myself by recalling fairly accurately the eloquent narration at that moving film's ending:

Eventually, all things merge into one, and a river runs through it. The river was cut by the world's great flood and runs over rocks from the basement of time. On some of the rocks are timeless raindrops. Under the rocks are the words, and some of the words are theirs. I am haunted by waters.[1]

Water is the impressionist painter God employs to craft the earth's geographical beauty. Jesus knew, and was in awe; he became one of us so we, too, might know and be in awe. Might he have whispered these words in Norman Maclean's ear?

Lisa and I had just spent days on the cliffs overlooking Yellowstone's twenty-four mile long, picturesque Grand Canyon, carved into majesty by the erosion of the Yellowstone River over more than a million years. And if you hike down to the Lower Falls overlook, the sound is deafening, and the sheer volume, the power of the water reminds me of Abraham Lincoln's dumbfounded response to visiting Niagara Falls. He was "staggered by the amount of water that fell—hundreds of thousands of tons per minute," and pondered "a corresponding marvel, that the sun had to lift just as much weight elsewhere, through constant, silent, undetected evaporation, followed by rainfall, to produce such a torrent." Then he mused,

> When Columbus first sought this continent—when Christ suffered on the cross—when Moses led Israel through the Red Sea, nay—nay, even when Adam first came from the hand of his Maker, then, as now, Niagara was roaring here....The mammoth and mastodon,...long dead,...gazed on Niagara. In that long time never still for a single moment. Never dried, never froze, never slept, never rested.[2]

Were Jesus's musings as he waded in the Jordan any less profound? Could our ponderings about water become more profound? Travel urges us to go on a long journey not just on the map, but in wisdom.

The whole spectacle of water, so much of it, flowing forever but so very fresh, so now, and the mind-boggling cause of the massive mountains and valleys that stand so solidly as mute witnesses to the power of what you can't cup in your own hand: so humbling, inspiring so much awe, maybe even faith in God.

In Grand Teton National Park, joined at the hip to Yellowstone, there is the cute little Chapel of the Transfiguration, fashioned of rustic, dark wood, but with a large clear glass window behind the altar giving worshippers a spectacular view of the Teewinot, Grand Teton, and Mount Owen (the Cathedral group). I'm happy never to have attempted to preach in such a place, as the trio of mountains over my shoulder would steal all the attention, a more eloquent witness to God's grandeur than any sermon could muster.

# Remember Your Baptism

If the flow of water over time can do all this, what might water do in you and me? How good of God to labor over creation so patiently with water, and to fashion our perceptions so we'd be dazzled by water. And thus, how good of God to plan things so that our first sacrament, our primal visible Word from God resides in the baptismal font. What could be more natural than the miraculous water that is a baptism? You, after all, are largely water, and you got your beginning in water. Before even your parents knew you had taken up residence in your mom's watery womb, God knew you were in there. You unwittingly posed for your first portrait via an ultrasound, which was first developed to detect icebergs and other sub-water mysteries.

In those magical moments just after you were born, you were almost 80 percent water. They gave you a bath, although you weren't dirty. You weren't dirty either when you were baptized, as an infant or as a big person. It was all about grace, as natural as water. Baptism announces to the world who you really are, and who all the others are as well, from Jesus wading into the Jordan to the holy host of the people of God who've been dunked in rivers and sprinkled at fonts in grand cathedrals or little rural A-frame chapels. Your true spiritual journey begins with this sacred water.

> *Baptism announces to the world who you really are, and who all the others are as well... Your true spiritual journey begins with this sacred water.*

We remind one another to "Remember your baptism," the unconditional grace, being enfolded into the people of God. Who brought you? Was it the one in whose womb you originally resided? And maybe dad too? No matter the quality, support, or frustration in your later relationship, you can bet that, in that moment, they were seeking blessing for you. Lucky parents see that blessing fulfilled over the years. For others, the blessing doesn't seem to happen. Hearts and lives are broken, and those parents feel like Isaac, realizing he was unable to bless Esau. Isaac "trembled violently" and Esau "cried out with an exceedingly great and bitter cry" (Genesis 27:33, 34). And yet the grace mysteriously is very much there.

Where were you baptized? I was baptized in a Baptist church in Dover, Delaware, after responding to an altar call that frightened the Hell out of me. I had no idea Pastor Adams would rather rudely shove my whole body under the water not once but thrice! That font, that pool, since that little church was drastically renovated years later, is now a storage closet for Bibles and children's Sunday school materials. I like that.

# The Wonder of Baptismal Fonts

Wherever I travel, I enter almost every church that's open and inspect the baptismal font. The very oldest surviving fonts are in Milan and Provence, eight-sided cavities dug into the floor, reminiscent of Roman baths, the ancient custom being that on Easter you took off your old, dirty work clothes, stepped down into the waters to be baptized, then stepped up and out to be wrapped in a brand new pure white robe and given a drink of milk and honey.

My favorite fonts? San Rufino, little visited but right there in a big square in Assisi, with unsurpassed bragging rights, having produced three saints: St. Francis, St. Clare, and in the nineteenth century, St. Gabriel, not to mention the emperor Frederick! Then we have the font in the sanctuary of Davidson United Methodist Church, crafted while I was pastor there. A large, beautiful glass bowl, featuring running water! When it was delivered, on day one, light from the afternoon sun streamed through a window, hit that glass bowl like a middle school science project, focused its energy on the carpet—and started a fire! So fitting.

We have many architectural wonders, like the stand-alone Baptistery of Florence, a twelfth-century octagonal marvel, with its stunning bronze doors by Ghiberti, where Dante was baptized. We have random rivers, ponds, and lakes where Christians have dunked or dipped new believers. Even indoors, we sing "Shall We Gather at the River." Everywhere is the Jordan.

And then, at Belmont Abbey, a short drive from my home, a stone that had been used as a trading block for slave auctions was repurposed into a marvelous font with a plaque attached that reads: "Upon this rock, men once were sold into slavery. Now upon this rock, through the waters of Baptism, men become free children of God." God admires this one. God made that rock a few billion years back. It lay around for a few millennia, then was put to perverse use that angered God. But then to God's giddy delight that old stone found its way into a church, held water for the thing Jesus told us to do to people, and now speaks to us.

The font is always the manifestation of considerable love and attention. We never use a plastic dog bowl; we never pour out of a sippy cup. The font is a work of art, however simple, a visual match for the work of art that is the water and the work of art that is the one being baptized. Speaking of which, years ago, I visited the Georgenkirche in Eisenach, Germany, where Johann Sebastian Bach was baptized on a wintry day in 1685. Four of his older siblings had already died of various causes. Alex Ross tried to imagine the scene: "I pictured Bach's parents looking on at the baptism, . . . and wondering whether he would live. They had no idea."[3] Indeed, as Ross thought this, he was listening to one of Bach's cantatas, recorded in that very church, three centuries after the baptism.

Baptism is about all of us living on, having a future with God, isn't it? And baptism is about our deep thirsts and desperate need for healing too, isn't it? The Bible is rich in stories and images of water slaking our deep thirsts and healing broken souls. Let's wade into a few.

# As a Hart Longs for Flowing Streams

The water coming out of the spigot, flowing under the bridge, or falling from the sky always comes from somewhere else. It has been on a journey, unseen. The Jordan River flows gently for most of its 150 miles. But not at the source. In the far north, in the shadow of snow-capped Mount Hermon along the Lebanese border, my pilgrim groups hike down ninety-five rocky steps to an astonishing, powerful waterfall at Banyas, formed from underground springs and the melting snow. The roar of the water, the mist pelting your face, the rapids coursing below: unforgettable.

My Old Testament professor at Duke, Roland Murphy, believed Psalm 42 was written there. Indeed: "from the land of Jordan and of Hermon, . . . at the thunder of thy cataracts" (vv. 6-7). When we arrive, I read the psalm over the din. "As a hart longs / for flowing streams, / so longs my soul / for thee, O God" (v. 1). In the dry, water-deprived land that is Israel, it's easy to imagine a deer, sniffing the air, coming to this lush, soaked place. A profound image of our parched souls.

It's not just thirst. There is clearly pain. "My tears have been my food / day and night, / while people say to me continually, / 'Where is your God?'" (v. 3). We cannot guess at the psalmist's trouble. You can fill in the blank with your own. The water we need, the water we are, the waters we shed in sorrow.

The waters rush toward the south, prompting this: "These things I remember, / as I pour out my soul; / how I went with the throng, . . . in procession to the house of God, / with glad shouts and thanksgiving, / a multitude keeping festival" (v. 4). As he thirsts for God in this place, he locates hope in the memory of being 150 miles to the south, far down river, in Jerusalem, at the Temple, among a vast crowd of those whose tears had been their food, thirsty for God. Knowing his solidarity with them, and the joy, blessing, and healing he and they had received in communal worship there made his soul overflow with joy and hope, even in such dense sorrow.

Fascinating: worship with the congregation fashions in us the sustaining we'll need when we're far away, in distance and in crisis. And the journey through the dry place is strengthened by the anticipated return to worship's holy place—which then makes the dry place holy. Everywhere is Jerusalem. The psalm's repeated refrain? "Hope in God." And the psalmist's resolution? "I shall again praise him, my help and my God" (vv. 5-6, 11). In pledging to praise God later, some small seed of praise has snuck in there already. Lovely. Perhaps that's what hope is.

Banyas, by the way, is an easy walk from Caesarea Philippi, which in Jesus's day featured a warren of Roman temples built to the deified Caesar, not to mention the Cave of Pan, the legendary "gate of hell," the proverbial entrance to the underworld. Today we clamber up some stone stairs and peer into the massive dark cavern that is this "gate of hell" and recall Jesus declaring the gates of hell would not prevail over his church, and asking, "Who do people say that I am? Who do you say I am?" The disciples were confused, as always.

It was here, in the far north, that Jesus turned his attention (as did the composer of Psalm 42) to the south, to Jerusalem. He explained that, yes, he was the One, and his destiny was to journey there and be handed over. I wonder if Jesus visited the waterfall. Surely he did. But did he ponder Psalm 42? Tears were his food. People asked him "Where is your God?" as they mocked. He even asked the same question on the cross! Of course, this Jewish man, who'd been to many festivals (like the psalmist), and in fact arrived to be killed at Passover, the greatest of the festivals, touched off a new festival, the one we call Holy Week, washing the disciples' feet, water gushing from his side from the soldier's lance. He's the one we're thirsty for.

# The Living Water of Jacob's Well

He is the Living Water. In another of the Bible's great stories fixated on water, Jesus told a woman at Jacob's well, "Every one who drinks of this water will thirst again, but whoever drinks of the water that I give will never thirst; it will become a spring of water welling up to eternal life" (John 4:13-14, my translation). That well is now situated underneath an Eastern Orthodox monastery on the outskirts of the politically perilous city of Nablus on the West Bank. It's hard to get there—for security reasons, but also due to the rocky terrain. Little skinny, narrow, winding roads test a driver's mettle; I've arrived there exhausted. John 4:4 reports that "[Jesus] had to pass through Samaria." But not because it was the easy or obvious route! Jesus "had to go" that way because he was on a mission, directed by God. The journey God calls us to follow is rarely the smooth, easy way.

> *The journey God calls us to follow*
> *is rarely the smooth, easy way.*

The well under that monastery, nearly three thousand years later, still functions as a well. The muscular caretaker lowers the bucket with a winch some 135 feet deep, finally pulls it all the way up, and pours the chilly, perfectly clear and tasty water into a cup for you to drink—from the same well from which Jacob, and then Jesus, and a holy host of others have drunk.

John 4 narrates a riveting, telling encounter Jesus has at this very well with a woman of Samaria. I'm not sure how best to characterize how Jews and Samaritans felt about one another. So close in their beliefs and practices! And yet they held one another in utter disdain, precisely because they were so close, and yet so far apart because of small matters of belief. Sound familiar?

So much in this story would have raised eyebrows in the ancient world. A man talking with a woman—alone! Oh my. And at noon. Most women retrieved their well water early in the morning or late afternoon. Did she come at noon to avoid other women, who might judge or snicker at her? She'd had five husbands and now lived with a man without being married. In ancient times, this would cause considerable tittering.

How startled was she when this holy rabbi didn't jump up and flee or scold her. He simply stayed, kept listening to her, showing her immense mercy she'd probably never experienced, ever. He felt neither pity nor smugness. He felt her pain. Her story of losing five husbands, no matter the details, whether death or desertion, reveals so much sorrow and grief. Her journey is into her past, where she is surprised, like us, to discover grace and welcome.

Jesus didn't even do the manly thing and draw the heavy bucket of water up for her. He asks her to do it. He trusts her. It's empowering, isn't it, when we don't do things for others, but watch and notice the beauty when they do for themselves, and do for others too.

Then their conversation goes symbolic, mystical. He trusts her to understand his profound reflection. There's water, but then he hints at "living water." He wryly points to the way you can drink now but you'll just be thirsty again in a while. "But whoever drinks of the water I shall give will never thirst; the water I give will become a spring of water welling up to eternal life." Thirst she knows—and we know. Jesus plays on that, and invites us to imagine, even daring to dream of not feeling so parched inside, of always having a rich resource, a flowing spring within, especially when times of agonizing thirst of the soul come to us.

Have you drunk from that well without knowing? All the water in the ecosystem that is our world migrates all over the place over the centuries. A raindrop falls, joins other drops feeding a stream flowing into a lake, where the water evaporates into a cloud which wafts its way over another place entirely, drunk by a little girl who perspires when she travels to grandpa's, all the water molecules circulating, on ice for a season in the Arctic, later in a steamy rainforest, seeping even later into Jacob's well but then your own town's drinking water.

Mystically but maybe literally, haven't we all drunk from this well of living water?

# Healing Waters

Water not only slakes our bodily and spiritual thirst. Water forgives and heals. The novelist Reynolds Price tells of a dream he had one night shortly after being diagnosed with a malignancy in his spine. Jesus was with him, wading in the Sea of Galilee, pouring handfuls of water over his head, saying "Your sins are forgiven." Price had the gall to say *"It's not my sins I'm worried about....* Am I also cured?"[4] We wish to be washed clean, but don't we long for more, tangible healing?

Galilee flows into the Jordan, whose waters people bottle and carry home in hopes of future healing. Consider 2 Kings 5, another of the Bible's great water narratives. Naaman "was a mighty man of valor. But..." (and there's always a *but*) "he was a leper." We can be sure he paid for help from the world's great healers. But it was a little girl, a slave who had come to him in the spoils of war, who knew to send him to Elisha, a modest prophet in a modest place. Naaman rumbled up to Elisha's little house with his chariot pulled by steeds, surrounded by his entourage. His emissary knocked on the door—but Elisha did not even come out. Instead he sent this mighty warrior a terse message: "Wash seven times in the Jordan" (my translation). The Jordan? That muddy creek? Naaman was appalled by this affront. They had impressive rivers where he'd come from. After his pride crumpled a bit, and maybe in desperation, he tiptoed into the Jordan, and got as wet and dirty as possible. When he stepped up onto the bank, drenched with water, "his flesh was restored like the flesh of a little child."

Our world features many places of pilgrimage and retreat with healing waters. Most famous may be Lourdes. In 1858, Mary appeared several times to a fourteen-year-old French girl named Bernadette Soubirous. Thousands of gallons of water flow from the spot where Bernadette interacted with Mary, and thousands claim to have been cured in the streams of the shrine there. In Turkey, my pilgrim groups always visit Pamukkale, with a landscape that looks like Mammoth Hot Springs in Yellowstone, its white travertine terraces formed by deposits from hot springs—which are said to cure many diseases.

My cure in Turkey came though just outside Ephesus at the house where Mary supposedly lived the last decades of her life. A spring just outside is reputed to have healing power. My hearing had nearly failed me that day, cause unknown. Skeptical of such things, I dipped my hand in the water, touched my ears—and immediately I could hear again. I thought, Nah...Maybe? Could it be?

If there are healing waters, we might ask what needs healing. I think of our family visit to Warm Springs, Georgia, home to President Franklin D. Roosevelt's "Little White House," where he stayed during his regular journeys south to swim and soak in Warm Springs's therapeutic mineral waters to ease his polio symptoms. Of course, he was there when he died, and they had to rush his longtime girlfriend, Lucy Mercer, away before his wife, Eleanor, arrived. A great man, of great suffering, and with great foibles.

# Geysers, Pools, and Other Dangerous Waters

Water evokes beauty, satisfaction, healing—and very real danger. Standing water in your basement, a dripping from the ceiling, a storm surge, even congestive heart failure: the perils of water. My mother had a brother who drowned when she was little. So to save me and my sister from drowning, she never let us near the water, which has ironically led to me nearly drowning a few times.

So, back to Yellowstone National Park, where this chapter began. It's nearly impossible not to reflect theologically on such a place. I have a good hunch that God even speaks powerfully to people who don't believe in God or never think twice about God in such a place. Your jaw drops here, there, everywhere in this dazzling theater of how massive, lovely, and downright weird God's creation can be, as if God decided to show off in a concentrated place for us to enjoy, and be in awe, and be extremely cautious.

The geysers: most of America's geysers are gathered along a strip of white sandy land, as if in a museum for comparison. No two are alike. Pent up heat, moisture, and pressure underground, unseen, finally erupt, and then settle, maybe like our emotions! Don't tiptoe too close to Yellowstone's downright bizarre waters: the Artist Paint Pots, laughably gurgling pits of mud, and all those multicolored, eerie pools that look like God's chemistry experiment, such as the Grand Prismatic Spring, the Morning Glory pool, the Emerald, and many more.

Signs warn that they are dangerous. The omnipresent rising steam happens because the temperatures soar upward to 200 degrees. But do humans heed the warning signs? When Lisa and I were driving about Yellowstone, we listened to an audiobook she'd downloaded called *Death in Yellowstone*, basically a compendium of dumb things people have done and lost their lives in the park. A selfie with a two-thousand-pound bison? Backing up to pose for just the right photo angle and falling? The hot waters: a man's dog jumped in, so he dove in to save his dog and lost his life. Countless others have decided to swim or wade and have lost life and limb. It's human nature: Don't eat this one fruit, and Adam and Eve went right for it. There's something essential in the spiritual life in simply heeding the signs. There's peril in the journey of faith. There's a cost to discipleship. You lose your life. You get swept up into something way beyond your control.

> *There's peril in the journey of faith. There's a cost to discipleship. You lose your life. You get swept up into something way beyond your control.*

When we got home, I read Megan Kate Nelson's *Saving Yellowstone*, the story of geologist and explorer Ferdinand Hayden leading a team of scientists, painters, and photographers to Yellowstone in 1871, not to discover what had always been there, but to map it and decipher how best to protect such a wonder of the world. It's a story of curiosity and courage, and yet perfidy, greed, and corruption. Native Americans, led by the Lakota chief Sitting Bull, were hounded, pushed out of their homelands and even killed, while financiers plotted get-rich schemes to take advantage of the place.

And so it goes with humanity. We protected Yellowstone and exploited it while ruining the lives of the innocents. The God whose artistic genius and unfathomable power created such a place must have mercy in equal measure when it comes to the people down here, like us. Water, after all, seems to be indifferent: it just flows, downhill, not choosing this or that to churn into, but lapping up on whatever bank or wader or rock it happens to come upon. The water is holy, but we can divert or pollute it into unholy uses. Pent-up whales in an amusement park, a wet t-shirt contest, or dumping toxic waste into a river: not fulfilling God's beautiful purpose for

God's precious water, but coercing the water, lacking its own free will, into an existence out of sync with God.

## Water Is Thicker than Blood

Finally, let's linger over the connections between the water and the people. "Blood is thicker than water" is a truism from the secular world. But with God, the creator of the water and the people, it's water that binds most profoundly. Rowan Williams suggested that "Baptism brings you into the neighbourhood of other Christians."[5] It's not that God promises to make your family happier or stronger. Jesus came into a family, but he did so to fashion a new family, a different kind of family not based on genetics or legalities, but on the one of whom Scripture says, "Out of his heart shall flow rivers of living water" (John 7:38).

Let's revisit that font in the cathedral, San Rufino, in Assisi. Francis's parents, Pietro and Pica Bernardone, brought him there for Holy Baptism. Their dreams for their son were not God's dreams. In that sacred moment, they were aiming for worldly success and popularity. Did they have any clue that the power of the Holy Spirit in the water applied might put those dreams at risk? Did they fathom sainthood might actually happen because of the promises they thoughtlessly muttered that day, and those the Spirit made with all intentionality? Didn't the power of the Spirit win the battle for his soul? And so Francis became St. Francis, abandoning his old, comfortable life, and living then with abandon for Christ and for Christ's poorest of the poor.

Back in medieval Assisi: with one stroke, Francis broke his parents' hearts, confirmed his oneness as a radical follower of Jesus, and started a family. Other young men he'd grown up with followed suit, abandoning their wealth and families. Francis called them "friars," which didn't mean holy men in a Catholic order, but simply "brothers." Women seemed to catch this contagion as well. Chiara Offreduccio, who would come to be known as St. Clare, sneaked out of her family's home on Palm Sunday night to join these brothers. Many sisters were soon to follow. Our spiritual journey discloses new, surprising, delightful siblings.

# The Holy Family

Jesus came not as an only child, but into a family, and he came not to save individual souls but to craft a new family. That family is amazing, quirky, confusing, messy, and mind-boggling; its beauty or ugliness are much debated, its creator long dead, and it seems it will never arrive at completion—much like the bizarre and fabulous church I took my daughters to visit in Barcelona: Sagrada Familia.

After an essential drugstore stop, we hurriedly visited the quirky *Casa Milà* and the *Casa Battló*, which make you feel you're in Disneyland instead of a neighborhood; and then the fun, elegant *Parque Güell*. Our minds were obviously transfixed by the peculiar artistry of the architect whose name is synonymous with Barcelona (well, unless soccer is your obsession): Antoni Gaudí. We were hustling in order to maximize our time at his church, Sagrada Familia.

There's nothing like it on planet earth. So massive and mind-boggling, you can't decide if you should gawk or chuckle, sigh or shudder. Awe is inevitable. And it's not even finished yet, although they started more than 140 years ago. Admission tickets yield $25 million a year, used toward its completion. And Gaudí, the genius behind it all, has been dead almost a hundred years.

I could feel exasperated by how long it's taking…but then again, it's a parable of how God's mystical church, God's holy family, is always under construction. Our personal journey into that family takes time. And I think of Reinhold Niebuhr's wisdom: "Nothing worth doing can be accomplished in a single lifetime; therefore we are saved by hope."[6]

The church is named for what is depicted on the Nativity Façade: the holy family. The whole idea of God incarnate, in a family like the rest of us, moves me. We may or may not all have children ourselves. But we are all the products of some family, small or large, healthy or kooky, the cauldron in which all of us came to be who we actually are. That God came to us in and through a family, albeit what we call the "sacred" family, is so hopeful, embodying, realistic.

I like to think about Jesus as a son and a brother in a family with the usual challenges, chores, and simple pleasures of keeping the fire tended, eating dinner, playing, squabbling, praying, embracing in the face of fear or loss. The Bible portrays almost all the families in its long, sprawling narrative as highly dysfunctional. Could Jesus—if he truly came to be one of us, one with us—have had a squeaky clean, entirely peaceful, healthy family? Didn't they have their moments? Mark 6:3 provides the names of some, but not all of his siblings: James, Joses, Judas, Simon, and his sisters (how many?) were left unnamed! All together in a one- or two-room house in Nazareth.

What more compelling witness could there be to the glory of Christ than that his own brother James became not just a Christian but the leader of the Church dedicated to the resurrection of his brother. If anyone could have said *Trust me, he's just a guy* . . . it would have been James.

Speaking of moments: Matthew 12:46-50 reports on the day Jesus was teaching and healing, and someone interrupted him to say, "Your mother and brothers are outside." We would expect him to have them ushered to seats of honor in the front! But Jesus replies, "Who is my mother, and who are my siblings? . . . Whoever does the will of my Father in heaven is my brother, and sister, and mother." Indeed, although we fawn over preachers and literature that promises Jesus will make our families swimmingly happy, Jesus pretty clearly came to forge a new family, not kin by blood but by God's Spirit—something profoundly hopeful for those from dysfunctional or broken families.

Gaudí, himself the youngest of five children, never married, never had little ones in his house or watching his work. For him, the Catholic community stood in as his family. There is a mystical expansiveness to the Holy Family. Jesus, James, and the others become our own siblings by water, theologically stronger than blood kinship. Some of us sense the need for such a family more than others. My nuclear family split, and I endured rough, fractured relationships with my parents until their deaths. I know I need family.

> The grace of God, the reality of God's church, doesn't bless our existing family so much as it creates a new sacred family. You're in. You belong. And you can't un-belong yourself, even if you duck or run.

But we all need this family, no matter how happy and secure our natural family might be. It's God's family. It's a wonder, complex and mystifying, like Gaudí's church. Mary, the one in whom God became flesh, is our mother. It's all mercy, all holiness, all hope. Pete Scazzero, as a feature of his program *Emotionally Healthy Spirituality*, coined the term "re-familying." You're in some family.

Own whatever it might be; you can and must stare directly at its truths, pains, blessings, wounds. The grace of God, the reality of God's church, doesn't bless our existing family so much as it creates a new sacred family. You're in. You belong. And you can't un-belong yourself, even if you duck or run. It's God's family, with love more unshakable and bonds more powerful than the noblest of all natural families.

# Everywhere Is Water

And so, in this whirlwind tour we've visited the Jordan, Yellowstone, South Georgia, eastern France, Assisi, along with a waterfall, a well, and a pool in the Holy Land. And we've barely tiptoed up to the Sea of Galilee, so important to Jesus and the disciples as we saw in the last chapter.

Isn't it intriguing that God came to a place where water is scarce, and therefore exceedingly precious? We without a thought can take water for granted. But in Israel, water was the ultimately valued commodity. So many texts are about drought, prayers for rain, Moses striking a rock, wadis that sometimes have water, sometimes not. God invites his parched (spiritually and physically) people to embark upon this journey: "Come, all you who are thirsty, come to the waters; you who have no money, come" (Isaiah 55:1 NIV).

Water, as God arranged things, is a lovely mystery, capable of much depth and rapid movement, tapped through fissures in rocks underground, floating like wispy cotton overhead, and even dazzling with color after the rain or at sunset. A snowflake is water. Jesus stood at the foot of Mount Zion, where the Spring Gihon flows from a hidden underground spot into the Pool of Siloam, where pilgrims were cleansed and the sick were cured, and said, "If anyone is thirsty, let him come to me and drink. He who believes in me: 'Out of his heart shall flow rivers of living water.' He said this about the Holy Spirit" (John 7:37, my translation). Indeed.

How would you name your deep inner thirst? What in you needs healing? What about you needs washing? If you could wade in the Jordan, or drink from Jacob's well, how could things change?

Where were you baptized? That is, where did it all begin? Yes, at your baptism, but even earlier: in the water of your mother's womb! God, who created all the waters, oceans, streams, and clouds, and fashioned us in water, and made us more than half water, sent his son Jesus, the Living Water, into the water of his mother's womb. He was baptized and told us to baptize and be baptized. And so what wiser counsel could there be than to "Remember your baptism"— even if you were just an infant. Caught in the rain? Remember your baptism. Taking a shower? Remember your baptism, and even ask to be washed, filled, and renewed right there in the shower. Washing dishes? As you care for each dish, pray for someone or something.

Everywhere is the Jordan. This elusive mystery reminds us that spirituality, the life of faith isn't just lying around obviously out in the open. You have to look, notice, and sniff the air like that hart. You have to ask for eyes to see, or fingers and feet to feel. You have to get outside. Go somewhere and find a stream, a pond, a storm cloud overhead. Stop near a bridge and get out of the car for a minute. Pull up images of a glacier or waterfall on your laptop. Join John Muir, the naturalist and intrepid explorer of Yellowstone, Yosemite, and other American wonders, in his life's mission: "As long as I live, I'll hear waterfalls and birds and winds sing. I'll interpret the rocks, learn the language of flood, storm, and the avalanche. I'll acquaint myself with the glaciers and wild gardens, and get as near to the heart of the world as I can."[7] And therefore as near to the heart of God.

And to your own heart. Look in the mirror. You look solid, but remember that what you see is almost two-thirds water! Barely holding together? God's grace. Staying hydrated? You already are. No wonder baptism is full of grace. No wonder a rain shower or watching waves lap onto the shore calms the soul. There's healing water in all the waters.

The healing, God making you into the one you are destined to be, takes time. How long ago did the mastodon gaze on Niagara? Or when did water begin to flow from Mount Hermon into the Jordan and into Galilee? You have a future with God. And you're in a family that lived for a time in Nazareth and will be around forever.

# CHAPTER 3

# Everywhere Is
# the Mount of Olives

## *Standing Up and Courage*

Palm Sunday: a fun morning in worship with children gussied up, processing down aisles toward the altar, waving green fronds giddily. "Tell Me the Stories of Jesus." "Into the city I'd follow the children's band, / waving a branch of the palm tree high in my hand"[1] Tim Rice shrewdly captured what was unfolding when he penned the lyrics for *Jesus Christ Superstar*: the crowd sings Hosanna and asks Jesus to smile, then in progression they ask "Won't you fight for me?" and finally "Won't you die for me?"

Pilgrim groups, including those I take, walk down, down, down (remember St. Francis going down, down, down?) the steep hill of the Mount of Olives, imagining Jesus bobbing along on the back of that donkey. But that walk isn't what it used to be. Back in the day, we would start in Bethany, where Jesus would have spent Saturday night with his friends Mary, Martha, and Lazarus, and walk about half a mile to Bethphage, at the crest of the Mount of Olives, and then down. But no more: in an attempt to solve Israeli-Palestinian tensions, a massive wall was erected, an extension of the one in Bethlehem, blocking the path. Humans at odds with God and one another: that's why Jesus made his way there in the first place.

So today we begin at the crest of the Mount of Olives, descending on a paved road (with the occasional motorcycle or taxi zipping by!), noting a massive Jewish cemetery on the left. Then trees and a handful of churches on the right, including the lovely teardrop-shaped *Dominus Flevit*, meaning "the Lord wept," recalling Jesus shedding tears over Jerusalem (Luke 19:41).

Past that teardrop, we weave further down the Mount of Olives. Close to the base of the Kidron Valley, we visit the garden of Gethsemane and the Church of All Nations, marking where Jesus prayed in agony after the Last Supper, and where he was arrested after Judas's kiss (Luke 22:40)—although on Palm Sunday, Jesus went right by and entered the city, probably through the East Gate, the "Golden" gate, which has for centuries been walled shut.

# Jesus's Immense Courage

Jesus was clearly making a point, one no one really understood. This was the day Pontius Pilate and his legions were marching into the city from Caesarea in the west, providing added military security to keep the peace in the thick of Passover, when tens of thousands of Jews, unhappy with the Romans, thronged into the city. Jesus came in from the east, the direction of the rising of a new day, the way the promised Messiah was expected to arrive—and he did so unarmed, riding not a war stallion but a meager donkey. The crowds pinned their fantasies of revolution on him, not yet understanding that his revolution was more radical than mere political power in a small country.

Such courage. He didn't sneak in under cover of night or by blending into the crowd. He didn't slide in on a random Tuesday, but at Passover, when dreams of political liberation clashed with clamped-down security—to underline that he didn't fit either paradigm. And location? He didn't ride a donkey into Las Vegas or Ireland. It was the Holy City with all its history and its future troubles—and Jesus invaded our world under the greatest of all the great emperors, as if to thumb his nose at all the powers then and now.

With no hint of egotism, he silently declared to the world, *Here I am*. He was calling the Romans out, along with those religious authorities who knuckled under to the lie that faith shouldn't confront the government but just get along. He was taking sides with the destitute and despised, the nobodies and the disenfranchised. Posing a laughable, alluring alternative to power, consumption, and intimidation, Jesus offered them and us peace, humility, love, and welcome. And Jesus wasn't done when the ride ended. I love Mark 11:11: Once the tumult of palm-waving and Hosannas settled down, "[Jesus] went to the temple. He looked around at everything and, as it was already late, went home to Bethany" (my translation). This is going to take some time...

Jesus came back the next day, Monday, same Palm Sunday walk, Bethany to Bethphage, down into and through the valley, and up into the Temple precincts. He knew his ride the previous day had rankled the authorities. But on Monday, he said *Here I am* more loudly. When my pilgrim groups climb the steps Jesus climbed into the Temple, we in awe recall the way Jesus shocked everyone by overturning the moneychangers' tables—not to condemn religious fundraising, but to symbolize the imminent overturning of all the old, corrupt ways of access to God. Courage indeed.

And as violent plans were being hatched to do away with him, Jesus didn't hide out, but came back on Tuesday to teach all day long—206 verses worth (Matthew 21–26). His words more than confirmed for the nervous political and religious authorities that he had no intentions of curtsying to them or fitting in; as "the chief priests and Pharisees" put it, "If we let him go on thus, the whole nation will follow him" (John 11:48).

On Thursday, he returned for the Passover meal, and then plunged out into the darkness to pray in Gethsemane, to bear Judas's betraying kiss, and then to be hauled off to a dark stone prison overnight before his mock trial and execution on the ironically named Good Friday—which we'll ponder more fully in chapter 6. But notice for now: he didn't run. He didn't hide. *Here I am. Here I stand.* Holy Week didn't surprise Jesus. He had decided in advance to make his stand. When? During his ministry? in the desert? at his baptism? as a boy?

What a week. Of the zillions of weeks since God designed our world, with time measured in such seven-day increments, this week was the most momentous, the truth and hope of all our weeks. It's the one week that is itself a huge ask for us on our journey: to make a decision, to take a stand.

# Here I Stand. God Help Me.

I took my daughter on a driving tour of Germany. We were looking for Bach, Bonhoeffer, and Martin Luther. In Wittenberg, Luther, this overly devout monk, was chagrined by the corruption he saw in church life. So, on October 31, 1517, he nailed his famous ninety-five theses to the church door. Religious authorities were appalled and began hounding him. He only doubled down, sparking the Protestant Reformation—whose shining moment came in 1521, in Worms.

Put on trial there before the most powerful men on the planet, Luther was shown a stack of books; they asked, "Are these yours?" With a bit of snark he replied, "They are all mine...and I have written more." "Will you repudiate all you have said?" What courage and resolve in Luther's reply: "My conscience is captive to the Word of God. I cannot and I will not recant anything....Here I stand. I cannot do otherwise. God help me."[2] I especially adore those last three words. The building in which Luther changed history is long gone, but a stone plaque, outdoors now, marks the spot. My daughter posed for a photo standing on that very spot—looking pretty darn cocksure.

Mind you, Luther was like most theologians, and even most Christians of his day in being appallingly anti-Semitic. And he created the worst church split in history, although his intention was reform, not division. Despite these disclaimers, we still have cause to admire his courage and zeal. There, in Worms, Luther stood.

On December 1, 1955, a diminutive seamstress (and a Methodist!) named Rosa Parks boarded a bus in Montgomery, tired after a day at work. A couple of white passengers got on, but she defied the rule that blacks move to the back or stand to yield their seats. The driver, James Blake, barked orders at her, but she didn't budge. Not Here I Stand, but *Here I Sit*.

# One of Us Should Stand with Her

Two years later, fifteen-year-old Dorothy Counts walked into Harding High School where I now live in Charlotte, alone, the first to integrate our all-white schools—a moment we mentioned back in chapter 1. As I look again at the photographs that captured the jeering, spitting, and rock-throwing to which she was subjected, I reflect on the courage she and her family mustered even to attempt

49

such a bold entry. Those images prompted James Baldwin to recover his courage: "One of us should have been there with her."[3] *Here I should have stood.* And he left Paris to enter the fray.

Way too often, we sanctimoniously chatter about "taking a stand," which is little more than passing judgment on somebody else. God asks us not to take a stand, but to stand—as in stand up, bodily, and with the one who's at risk, who's being mistreated unjustly. Surprisingly enough, that's often enough in our journey toward God and others. When George Floyd was killed, I phoned my black pastor and laity friends, and went and just sat with a couple of them. When there's an anti-Semitic incident, I call rabbis and a couple of other Jewish friends just to say, "I am with you." That's what Jesus promised so marvelously: "I am with you always" (Matthew 28:20).

> *God asks us not to take a stand,*
> *but to stand—as in stand up, bodily,*
> *and with the one who's at risk,*
> *who's being mistreated unjustly.*

The mandate isn't to be a Christian in the privacy of our souls, or in church with people like us. Just as God chose to stand with us in our humanity, we keep an eye out for moments when we can stand *with*. Our journey? Get off the couch, out of the house and the church, and we go and stand.

Part of the holy value of travel is the inevitable testing of your ethical mettle. If I'm on my couch at home, or at the club, or at a resort, nothing much is asked of me morally, or societally. Courage isn't required. Maybe that's why people love home, club, and resort. But if I am standing at Oskar Schindler's grave in Jerusalem, I have to ask myself what I would do, at great risk to my own safety, for the Jews or whatever group of strangers are under threat. If I am in Memphis, Graceland doesn't ask much of me. But the Lorraine Motel asks me if racism is really a thing of the past in me, and what God might want of me and other people of faith in the ongoing labor to ensure no one is marginalized because of anybody's prejudice. I don't ask that in my own back yard.

Where do we stand next? And with whom? The news, which so easily becomes a litany of disasters to get worked up into an ideological lather over, or more often cause to avert our gaze, can be God's call—as James Baldwin learned. When Russia invaded Ukraine, I reached out via denominational connections, kept making phone calls, and finally wound up talking with a United Methodist pastor in Poland whose congregation was hosting refugees. In a Zoom conference call with a handful of Ukrainians, I simply shared that we were praying for them, that many people I knew were flying Ukrainian flags and had yard signs saying, "We stand with Ukraine." This shocked and delighted them. They had no idea people so far away would care. A simple gesture of solidarity made a world of difference.

We are peppered with news stories and political pontification about immigrants at the border. Which side should the Christian be on? We begin not by taking a stand, but standing with those most impacted. It wasn't hard for my church people to get to McAllen, Texas, and offer food, drink, compassion, and conversation with immigrants, none of whom fit the stereotypes, all of whom were exhausted, desperate, and deeply moved by the simple fact that we showed up and interacted with them as precious children fashioned in God's image, instead of as political pawns or targets of fear-mongering rage. Talk about being on a journey: theirs might inspire ours!

# Good Trouble Crossing a Bridge

I'm a lucky dog to have walked across some of the world's great bridges: the Pont Neuf in Paris, the Charles Bridge in Prague, Ponte Vecchio in Florence, and London's Tower Bridge. I love covered bridges, my favorite being in Gay, Georgia—and the Congress Avenue Bridge in Austin, Texas; thousands of bats fly out from underneath at sunset every day.

The most emotionally moving bridge crossing though, for me, came in Selma, Alabama. I had read about "Bloody Sunday" in March 1965, and I had been moved by Ava DuVernay's film *Selma*, starring David Oyelowo. But on our Deep South pilgrimage our church embarked on in 2019, I got to walk across the Edmund Pettus Bridge with my wife and my longtime friend, Richard Harrison. There's something about walking on a sacred place with family, and in this case with an African American friend for whom Selma defined his childhood, and America's lunge toward transformation. Richard wept as we walked. He loved to say "February is Black History Month? Every month is Black History Month—and it's not Black History; it's OUR History."

On Bloody Sunday, marchers were gassed and beaten. John Lewis, who later served thirty-three years in Congress, nearly died. In 2005, he and hundreds of others crossed the bridge once more, with Lewis noticing that "it's gratifying to come back and see the changes that have occurred."[4] Presidents George Bush and Barack Obama have joined in anniversary marches.

Lewis was the one Richard, Lisa, and I talked about after we crossed the bridge. It wasn't Lewis's first time being physically brutalized while peacefully striving for equality. He'd been beaten within an inch of his life as a teenager in Nashville. Years later someone showed him a photo of himself, so young, emerging from jail, swollen and bloodied still. Observing his own confidence, he said, "I had never had that much dignity before.... It was exhilarating."[5]

Years later, as the senior citizen of the civil rights movement, Lewis famously spoke God's prophetic word to us all: "Speak up, speak out, get in the way.... Get in good trouble, necessary trouble, and redeem the soul of America."[6] After Lewis died, pressure mounted to rename the bridge for him. But it's named as it should be: Edmund Pettus was a Civil War hero, and then a Grand Dragon of the Ku Klux Klan. It was that bridge, and all Pettus and his ilk stood for, that was crossed.

There's something in the journey of faith about crossing bridges, building bridges, and even being a bridge. The Latin word for "priest," *pontifex*, means bridge-builder. That's what a priest, a pastor—and even a regular lay Christian—does: she or he is a bridge between people and God, between the challenges of the world and the life of God. We never settle for passing judgment. We strive as valiantly as possible to build a bridge, always, to connect, to find together our way toward God.

Jesus was the ultimate bridge-builder and bridge-crosser. St. Catherine of Siena, in the fourteenth century, thought of the wood of the cross of Christ and imagined that wood as a bridge between God and us. Jesus reconciled us to God so we might be reconciled to one another. So countercultural!—in our society where everybody's mad at somebody.

# Saint Francis, Courageous Peacemaker

Time with Francis of Assisi is always well-spent. Superficially he strikes most people as a sweet, gentle figure, with birds fluttering about his statue in flower gardens. But Francis was a person of immense courage. To shed the wealth and security of home, to bolt from the love of his parents, to embrace lepers all required startling courage. He strode into the palace of the pope, daring to suggest the hope of the church wasn't in pomp and power but in humility and poverty. And then he went to Egypt...

Talk about a journey! Saint Francis joined the heavily armed Crusaders on their vengeful expedition to slaughter Muslims. At Damietta, near the Nile, both sides readied for battle. Francis, unarmed, walked across the No Man's Land separating the armies. They drew their sabers—but he looked so pitiful, so meek, a curiosity. Did he say, *Here I stand? Here I am?* They led him to the Sultan, Malik al-Kamil. They spent three days together, becoming friends—and the army withdrew for a time.

Then there's a story I believe, despite its fairy tale feel. Francis went to Gubbio, about an hour's drive north of Assisi, and found the city gates locked. He discovered the citizens were being terrorized by a wolf up in the hills, who'd eaten a few folks. Posses had failed to apprehend him. Francis said, "I must go and speak with my brother Wolf." Unarmed he walked up into the hills. The citizens of Gubbio watched from the top of their walls, fearing for him.

The wolf emerged, snarling. Francis made the sign of the cross, and the wolf sat down. Francis said "My brother, you have sinned against God by harming these people. But I understand why you did so. There's clearly no food up in these hills. You were hungry. If you repent and promise to stop, I will get the citizens of Gubbio to promise to feed you for the rest of your life." The wolf lifted his paw, which Francis shook.

He led the wolf into the city. The people were jittery at first, but over time they grew to love the wolf. Instead of running at him with knives, they gave him porridge. When he died, they grieved. Archaeologists found, some six hundred years later, a small ornate casket buried under the cathedral—with the bones of a wolf.[7]

Francis was always and everywhere simply trying to replicate the life of Jesus, to see if Jesus might actually be here, there, wherever Francis was. *What would Jesus do?* can be an innocuous question if plastered on a t-shirt or poster, or etched on jewelry, and worn by people who've not looked very carefully into the things Jesus actually did. Whom did he touch? Whom did he offend? Why was he so polarizing? People doggedly followed him any- and everywhere, while others were mortified and couldn't wait to rid the world of him. We perceive Jesus as gentle, kind, even a man of sorrows—and rightly so. But can we begin to grasp how very courageous he was? And how he boldly, again and again, stood in places of great risk, and with all the wrong people?

> *We perceive Jesus as gentle, kind, even a man of sorrows—and rightly so. But can we begin to grasp how very courageous he was? And how he boldly, again and again, stood in places of great risk, and with all the wrong people?*

# As for Me and My House

Jesus was unique, and Luther, Francis, Counts, Parks, and Lewis were special. Yet they were reiterating what God's people had always done. Noah hammered away on his big boat, no doubt bearing the mockery of his neighbors. Abraham showed up with his young beloved son Isaac, ready to do whatever God asked of him, even if it was the worst conceivable ask for him. Joseph revealed himself to his brothers, who'd tried to do him in, saying literally *Here I am, your brother, Joseph*—and he forgave them. Job never ceased from crying out to a seemingly absent and possibly cruel God, showing up repeatedly, asking God to stand up and answer. Jeremiah stood up for God and was ridiculed by family and friends.

Near Jacob's well, where Jesus stood with the Samaritan woman (John 4) is the small village known in Bible times as Shechem. Roughly twelve hundred years before Jesus befriended that Samaritan woman there, Joshua (Moses's successor) gathered all the tribes of Israel, forty years removed from Egyptian slavery, and made one of the Bible's great speeches. A challenge. An invitation— to them, and to us.

As a kid, I was given the impression that the Israelites rolled into the Promised Land and, like a German Blitzkrieg, conquered the whole region. We didn't need fancy scholarship to show us otherwise. Mark the conquered places on a map. They didn't win much ground at all, and what territory they captured was not the most fertile. There were Canaanites all over the place, wealthier, with more power, and a religion that lured Israelites repeatedly into idolatry.

Knowing the challenges to come, Joshua (in the book named for him, in chapter 24) rattles off a profound history lesson of how they got there, going back to Abraham, into days of cruel slavery in Egypt, through decades of wilderness wanderings, God sticking with them despite their foolishness. Noting a veritable mall of other gods that would be peddled on them, he urges them, "Fear the Lord. Serve him faithfully. Put away the other gods. Choose this day whom you will serve. As for me and my house, we will serve the Lord "(my translation).

I've stood in that field where he uttered such words. Wherever you stand or sit, right now, you have to make a decision, and a hard, serious one. It's not some vague spirituality or sliding into a pew now and then. Choose your God or your gods! Take a stand; make this journey—and live it, with courage, grit, patience, maybe making that definitive decision again. And again.

# Give Me That Bible Stuff

My children love to razz me in front of other parents by saying, "Dad never took us to Disney World." I think there's an undertone of pride in their kidding. We did make it to Disney's neighbors, Sea World and Universal Studios, so don't get the wrong idea. And yet I did invest time taking them to places where somebody was noble, where a woman or a man managed to be the best we all are capable of being.

I took my son to ride the roller coasters at Universal Studios. On the way, we stopped off at the Jimmy Carter childhood home in Plains, Georgia, but more importantly at its neighbor, ten minutes away, just outside Americus: Koinonia Farm.

Everybody has heard of Habitat for Humanity, in virtually every city in America, and now worldwide in scope. Saints you know have hammered on houses—and perhaps even lived in a Habitat house too. It started because a wealthy man, trying to fix his flailing marriage, went on vacation with his family, and had been encouraged to stop by a place in the middle of nowhere in Georgia to meet a saint. Instead of staying for lunch, he stayed for a month, and then came back for a lifetime. Millard Fuller wound up giving away his wealth—a bit like St. Francis—and launching Habitat, which has built millions of homes.

The saint he met who changed everything? A quirky, smart, smart-alecky farmer-preacher named Clarence Jordan. Clarence grew up Baptist, and as a child proved to be one of those souls with a natural sensitivity to hypocrisy.

He was confused by his church singing "Red and yellow, black and white, they are precious in his sight" while black children were shabbily dressed. One night, he even happened upon some church deacons torturing a black man on a rack, the same deacons he'd sat with in worship singing of their love for Jesus.

He studied agriculture in college, attentive to the plight of poor farmers. He couldn't get over the clash he felt between his ROTC commitment and the plain words of Scripture. Could a soldier follow Jesus, who told us to love our enemies? These and other agonies of conscience led him to enroll at Southern Baptist Theological Seminary in Louisville, Kentucky, where he earned one more degree, a doctorate in Greek New Testament. Later he would become famous for his homespun renderings of the New Testament, the funny and provocative *Cotton Patch Version*.

But his most brilliant translation of the New Testament did not appear in print, but in his real work on the red earth of Georgia. In 1942, Jordan founded Koinonia Farm, near the county seat town of Americus. Koinonia enfleshed his dream of the kind of community portrayed in the Book of Acts (2:42-45, 4:32-36), in which fellowship (*koinonia* in Greek) involved communal sharing of all goods—not to mention blacks and whites living together. In those days, fine church people in the South weren't remotely ready for this type of living out of the Gospel. Jordan and his Farm were constantly under assault. The Ku Klux Klan terrorized, vandalized, and firebombed Koinonia.

You can visit Koinonia, as my son and I did. I parked in their dirt lot, but immediately walked back to the highway, remembering that when Dorothy Day had come to visit, she was photographed sitting at the end of the driveway. And she also was shot at by the Klan! There's a fairly spartan dorm where you can sleep for a mere donation, and a refectory where meals are shared. Further into the property, we found "Clarence's shack," a little green structure where he penned those *Cotton Patch* versions, studied, and prayed. We walked the length of the property, and I told my son stories about Clarence.

One Sunday in 1948, Jordan brought a dark-skinned man (actually an Indian) to the local church. The deacons insisted Jordan meet with them and refrain from causing trouble. Jordan handed a Bible to one of them, saying "Show me where it says in the Book that if a man is dark-skinned, he should not enter the house of the Lord." The deacon angrily handed the Book back, while another shouted "Brother Jordan, don't pull that Bible stuff on us!" Jordan's reply? "I'm asking you to give it to me." He loved to say that on that day he and his friends became "ex-Baptists."

After one of many intimidating attacks from the KKK, when asked why he didn't just give up, Jordan declared, "It was not a question of whether or not we were to be scared, but whether or not we would be obedient." We should ponder that when Christians stand up for and with someone, there can be painful repercussions for their families. Not surprisingly, Clarence's family suffered much. His daughter Jan was ridiculed at school, especially by a vicious boy named Bob Speck, who called her ugly names and threw her books on the floor over and over. Hearing about this, Clarence grew angry to the point he told Jan, "I'm coming to school tomorrow. I've tried to be a follower of Jesus, and he taught me to love my enemies and all that, but I'm going to ask Jesus to excuse me for about fifteen minutes while I beat the hell out of Bob Speck." Jan said, "Daddy, you can't be excused from being a Christian for fifteen minutes."[8]

# Unrevealed Until Its Season

It's the commitment never to take a fifteen-minute break that makes courage necessary. But it needn't mean you try to get yourself harmed. Jesus was warned Herod was out to get him, but he bided his time until the right time. After Luther uttered his famous "Here I Stand," he went into hiding for a season. He grew a beard, took a fake name (Junker Jörg), and lived in the Wartburg Castle, which looms high on a cliff above Eisenach, Bach's birthplace. It was there, in 1522, battling depression, ill health, constipation, and violent mood swings, that Luther translated the Bible into German—in eleven weeks! I have stood in that small wooden room which still houses Luther's desk where this grand achievement in the history of civilization happened.

The Reformation was spreading like wildfire—but he could not have known how the face of the world would change because of what he did, day by day, in that cold room at that desk. Of course, German, as a language, was in its infancy; the brilliant Renaissance genius Erasmus observed that "this Bible did more than any other book to shape German and German literary style." How lovely that the Bible served as the foundation of a modern language! But more importantly: making the Bible available to regular people not privileged to have learned Latin, like the priests, forever altered how people such as us own Bibles and read them for our own personal edification. Peasants, merchants, tradesmen, laborers, and the elderly were hungry to study pages of Bible they could understand. We may have good cause, thinking of their eagerness, to feel a bit embarrassed when we let our readily available Bibles sit around the house unopened.

> *Making the Bible available to regular people not privileged to have learned Latin, like the priests, forever altered how people like us own Bibles and read them for our own personal edification.*

Luther understood how Bible mattered—and music also. He wrote hymns, such as "A Mighty Fortress Is Our God," which can itself stir much courage in us simply by singing it! With "the right man on our side," "we will not fear." "The prince of darkness grim"? "We tremble not for him." Indeed, "The body they may kill." Here we stand.

A marvelous travel memory: my daughter Sarah and I were poking around in the Augustinian monastery in Erfurt, Germany, where Martin Luther figured out who he was and what God was asking of him. We stumbled upon a tour group; their guide was explaining that we were in the very room where Luther and the monks worshipped every day. Stone, medieval, live acoustics: a lovely place. Without any warning, or anyone saying anything at all, when there was a moment of silence, the tour group began spontaneously to sing "A Mighty Fortress Is Our God" with much emotion, even tears. When they were done, I found out they were recently retired Lutheran pastors who'd dreamed all their lives of coming to this place and singing this hymn, their hymn.

We could devote an entire book to the relationship of music and courage, of the way people singing together stirs some higher unity and noble purpose we can't achieve just by talking. I love the notice in the Gospels that, at the Last Supper, Jesus and the disciples sang together—and we know from Jewish tradition that they would have sung Psalms 113 through 118. What stirred in Jesus's heart as they sang "The snares of death encompassed me," "I will lift up the cup of salvation," "Precious in the sight of the LORD is the death of his saints," or "With the LORD on my side, I do not fear"? I wish I'd been born soon enough to have marched in the sixties and sung "We Shall Overcome." I strain to overhear voices on southern plantations singing "Swing Low, Sweet Chariot," emboldening them not to wait on heaven but to get on board that "Gospel Train" to freedom.

# The Day the Phone Rang

Luther fled and hid. Slaves defied their masters; they fled and hid. Courage isn't simply bearing whatever sufferings come your way. There's discretion. Jesus was hounded by Herod for months before his time finally came to force things. And then, when discretion fails and those who stand suffer or are even killed: what is the disposition of those who stand?

So to Bonhoeffer: as a young man, I fell in love with this giant of a theologian who was executed by the Nazis just days before the end of World War II. He would have gone down in history as one of the church's greatest thinkers without the whole opposition to Hitler thing. But his courage in the face of lethal threats from the Gestapo, and leading other pastors and their churches into peril to stand against evil: so moving, and for a man who grew up in a fairly comfortable home among professional people.

Like James Baldwin in Paris, Bonhoeffer was safely ensconced in London and then America but knew God wanted him back in the thick of the troubles in his home country. In the concentration camp, he wrote unforgettable letters. "We have to learn that personal suffering is a more effective key, a more rewarding principle for exploring the world in thought and action than personal good fortune." "We can have an abundant life, even though many wishes remain unfulfilled." "Nothing that we despise in the other man is inherently absent from ourselves. We must learn to regard people less in the light of what they do or omit to do, and more in the light of what they suffer."[9] Bonhoeffer understood how our personal goodness can block doing God's will, that God doesn't ask us to keep our hands clean, but to get them dirty doing God's work.

My visit to his home was unforgettable. First, my guide took me upstairs to Bonhoeffer's bedroom. Wooden bookshelves lined two walls. He'd built them with his own hands for his books by Luther and a holy host of other theologians who shaped his thinking. By the window was his small desk and chair, where he wrote his books—and you have to consider when he sat there, he was probing the heart and mind of God and writing down what he was hearing, visualizing, understanding. So beautiful. Downright inspired, and inspiring. And of course, his harpsichord next to his desk. He loved music, especially Bach.

My guide walked me down the stairs. At the bottom, we stopped by an old-timey phone sitting on a stand. He told me of the day this phone rang, and a Nazi sympathetic to Bonhoeffer called to say, "Get out of the house now, run, now." Bonhoeffer ran upstairs to grab his bag, and as he got to the door, the Gestapo was already there. They seized him and took him away. His parents, siblings, and fiancée never saw him again.

That phone at the bottom of the stairs is etched deeply inside me, as is the cell at Buchenwald I got to visit where Bonhoeffer was incarcerated, and where he won the affection and admiration of even the most brutal Nazis. They were moved by his calm, his hospitable spirit, a palpable joy in the face of the worst. The camp physician wrote: "In the almost fifty years I worked as a doctor, I have hardly ever seen a man die so entirely submissive to the will of God."[10]

We could say more about Germany. The Holocaust lingers and haunts the landscape there. Within the lifetime of many still living there, Jews and a few Christians were murdered out of unadulterated, vile hatred among Lutherans and Catholics who were faithful churchgoers. But Germany has done sensible things. Freedom of speech generally reigns in Germany, but you cannot fly a Swastika flag or promote anything kin to Nazism; and Hitler's apartment in Berlin is unfindable. They understand how horrific some expressions of freedom can be, how dangerous, so atrocious that their state says *This cannot be here.* Are God's people called to defy hurtful expressions targeting victims of prejudice?

We've ventured to several places where Christians simply stood, with courage and at considerable cost. Shouldn't we think more often of the ways the life of faith involves courage? Faith isn't the refuge of the fearful. Hearing and responding to God's call, and living a holy life that matters in the world, requires courage—precisely because God is good and has created so much wonder. In her courage-inducing novel *Gilead*, Marilynne Robinson writes,

> Theologians talk about a prevenient grace that precedes grace itself and allows us to accept it. I think there must also be a prevenient courage that allows us to be brave—that is, to acknowledge that there is more beauty than our eyes can bear, that precious things have been put into our hands and to do nothing to honor them is to do great harm.[11]

Do you have any time? or a way to get around? or a phone? Go where Jesus has already gone ahead of you. Stand with him, and with the vulnerable, the wounded with whom he stands.

# The Passion to Be One with Jesus

There's one more harrowing thing, one with a surprising, exquisite beauty. This proximity to Jesus, this desire to be one with him, requires a peculiar courage, perhaps best exemplified in a little-noticed episode late in the life of St. Francis. It happened at LaVerna, a place in Tuscany, seemingly light years from the glories of the *dolce vita* of Florence, Siena, Cortona, or Lucca.

A long, steep, narrow (and scary) road winds its way up the mountain to a complex of modest buildings marking a haunting, mysterious moment in Francis's life. Over the years, Francis had become obsessed with the crucifixion of Jesus, with his suffering for us. Often people would find him standing by the road, weeping. Why? He was simply thinking as he walked along of Jesus's agony on the cross, of Jesus's intense love, of Jesus's physical pain—and was overcome with grief. He scarcely wanted to think of much else.

Two years before his death, Francis withdrew from the crowds to the precipitous cliffs and hanging caves of LaVerna. I have taken quite a few groups there myself. According to legend, Francis was climbing the mountain and collapsed in exhaustion and thirst. Miraculously, water spouted from the rocks and a flock of birds gathered to sing. Francis climbed higher. Scrambling over crevices and boulders in this craggy terrain, Francis imaginatively felt he was entering the wounds of Christ; some call LaVerna "a wounded mountain." Francis believed that the earthquakes that accompanied the crucifixion of Christ rippled all the way to Italy to create this rugged landscape.

And so, on this wounded mountain, Francis envisioned Jesus on the cross and prayed intently, with words of unmatched theological power:

> My Lord Jesus Christ, I pray You to grant me two graces before
> I die: the first is that during my life I may feel in my soul and in
> my body, as much as possible, that pain which You, dear Jesus,
> sustained in the hour of Your most bitter Passion. The second is
> that I may feel in my heart, as much as possible, that excessive
> love with which You, O Son of God, were inflamed in willingly
> enduring such suffering for us sinners.[12]

What happened next is either sheer miracle or some horribly
flawed fabrication. An angelic seraph, nailed to a cross—or was it
Christ himself?—flew down and pierced the hands, feet, and side
of Francis. For the remaining two years of his life, he was marked
by these wounds, the "stigmata." Although he tried to hide them,
a few friends caught a glimpse now and then. The wounds bled
intermittently, but Francis never complained. When his corpse
was prepared for burial, the *stigmata* were uncovered and certified
as genuine. Since that time, history has known other "stigmatics,"
holy believers who suffer medically unexplainable wounds in their
hands, feet, and sides that bleed periodically.

LaVerna's Chapel of the Relics exhibits a tablecloth, bowl, and
cup Francis used when he was there. A small piece of linen is thought
to be stained with Francis's own blood; and then there is the very
garment Francis wore when he received the stigmata. I check the
time when we visit, because at 3 p.m. sharp, every day, the monks
gather in the large sanctuary, chant their prayers, and then walk
together (and they invite us to join them!) in a holy processional
down a long concourse to the place where Francis received the
stigmata. Unforgettable.

Paul spoke obliquely about carrying "the marks of Jesus" on his
body (Galatians 6:17). To be marked with Jesus: it is as if Jesus wrote
"What wondrous love is this?" onto the very body of Francis. Why

was Francis chosen for this miracle? Was his devotion to Christ more passionate than mine? Do I want to go so far? Do I want my heart to be broken by the things that break the heart of God? Do I want to share in God's pain? Such questions!—for us who avoid suffering at all costs. But does it cost us? We never know the heart of God, and the profound love of God, until we enter into his wounds.

To ask *What would Jesus do?* begins and ends in What *did* Jesus do? Jesus let himself be treated brutally. He was mocked, slapped, flogged. He let his holy, beautiful body endure the most gruesome physical torment of crucifixion. Large iron nails were driven through his flesh and bone into a shaft of olive wood. A lance pummeled his abdomen. Thorns pressed into his forehead.

I am not sure if I dare pray Francis's prayer. Then again, is asking God for comfort—a reasonable ask!—really the way to draw close to and love our Savior?

# CHAPTER 4

# Everywhere Is Bethlehem

## *Prayer Walls*

I've never seen the Great Wall—the one occupying the name "Great"—in China. But I've seen some impressive, historic walls: Hadrian's Wall, the Vietnam Memorial in Washington, the Berlin Wall (what little is left of it), not to mention Troy, Jericho, and Istanbul. Medieval Assisi was and is walled. Francis shocked his family by choosing the insecurity of living outside those safe walls. I had a grumpy neighbor who built a wall around his yard to keep kickballs and children out. Some neighbors of mine erect a cool pumpkin wall every Halloween. A wall can be lovely, but more often a wall is a mute witness to unresolved troubles, a show of strength not cloaking the fear behind it very well.

## Wailing Walls

In our introduction, we touched on a massive wall in the land of modern Israel designed to separate Israelis and Palestinians.

69

Whether you view it as a needed security barrier or a gross injustice verging on apartheid, the wall is silent testimony to intense strife. Its most dominant, ominous section is, paradoxically, right there in Bethlehem, the birthplace of the one whose mission was to tear down "the dividing wall of hostility" (Ephesians 2:14).

But there is a surprising loveliness to that ugly wall, marked as it is with beautiful signs of hope: fabulous graffiti, none of it mean or stirring violence, every image a vision of peace. A soldier tossing, not a grenade but a bouquet of flowers. The roots of the tree of life bulging under the wall, creating cracks and openings. A dove of peace, olive branch in its beak, but wearing a flak jacket. "Make hummus, not walls." And story boards, where mothers tell of tragedies that befell their husbands and sons. I like to envision all that graffiti as a prayer, a plea, many pleas to God and anyone who will listen.

Just five miles north of Bethlehem, you find yourself in the heart of old Jerusalem, standing in a wide, paved plaza facing another wall: the Western Wall of the Temple Mount—the one remaining fragment of stone wall in Bible times not destroyed by the Romans, sacred to Jews, and all faiths, often known as the "wailing wall." Tourists and regulars pray facing the wall, and jam prayers on little pieces of paper into the crevices between the massive stones. I've done this dozens of times. Moves me every time. And hopefully it moves God.

I once saw a woman praying at the Wall—not at the outdoor plaza, but in the underground tunnel, in the dark, at the very point we think is closest to the ancient Holy of Holies. Israelis don't call the wall "wailing" anymore, but that's what this woman was doing. Her Bible was open, pressed with her right hand against her face, getting soaked with her tears, which I saw trickling toward the ground. Her body was bobbing, oscillating; her sobs were harrowing. I wanted to tap her on the shoulder and find out what troubled her so, or what passage her Bible was open to, or comfort her. I felt a bizarre twinge of envy. Have I ever prayed so zealously, so agonizingly, so intimately?

My favorite character in Sue Monk Kidd's *The Secret Life of Bees* is May, whose twin sister April had died. They had been "like one soul sharing two bodies. If April got a toothache, May's gum would plump up red and swollen." After April's death, "it seemed like the world itself became May's twin sister."[1] Any word of anyone suffering struck agony into May's heart; she was constantly heartbroken. All her family could do was build a "wailing wall" in the back yard; May would write down the hurts of the world and people she knew on scraps of paper and press them into the wall. Everywhere is Jerusalem.

In our world defined by too many walls, where the very word *wall* is shrilly politicized, I ponder the Bethlehem graffiti, and the wall in Jerusalem, a wall Jesus would have seen and touched, at a place where he prayed and called all of us to account for our rancor, greed, divisions, and all other manner of sin, a wall he passed by and through struggling under the weight of his cross. Don't these walls invite us to draw close, to be like one soul, a twin sibling, with God and what aches in God's heart—and to share in not just God's brokenness but that of all who are shut out, or who are so scared they try to shut others out? Isn't this where the journey of prayer leads?

# Jesus in Montgomery and Gethsemane

Wailing happens, and in so many places. God, who deigns to be our twin, comes down, and what happened in one holy place unfolds once again in a very different place that turns out not to be so different at all. I love to linger in the kitchen of the Dexter Avenue Baptist Church parsonage in Montgomery, Alabama. The stove, refrigerator, and little table in the middle are old school, so we can get the feel of the place where young Dr. Martin Luther King Jr. and his wife, Coretta, ate, cooked, talked, and prayed. I fixate on it because of one night in January 1956, not long into the Montgomery bus boycott. King, his supernova of leadership rising, had endured the firebombing of his parsonage, and constant death threats.

Then came the moment the phone rang at midnight. Another vile threat. Unable to sleep, he made coffee, sat at that kitchen table, and felt he "couldn't take it any longer." Then God spoke to him—to "stand up for the truth, stand up for righteousness"— with the reassurance that "I will be with you until the end of the world."[2] See how what happened in the Holy Land manifests itself across space and time? Jesus had reassured his beleaguered, fearful disciples just before his ascension (Matthew 28:20), and then he spoke those same words to an exhausted, trembling King in his place of direst need.

Speaking of wailing: my pilgrim groups visit the garden of Gethsemane by day, but it was dark when Jesus was there. Was there a little moonlight? Or was it a cloudy night? This "garden" is more of a small grove of olive trees. Some in that grove today are fifteen hundred years old, and they sprouted from the residual roots of the trees under which Jesus prayed. Those haunting, gristled, knotty trees looked like what Jesus was experiencing in his gut: agony (some manuscripts of Luke included the note that his perspiration was "like great drops of blood," Luke 22:44), pleading with God his Father to let him elude the cruel, gruesome death that was drawing close. Could he have said *No*? Wouldn't God have shown mercy to his beloved Son if he'd slipped away to safety?

Jesus made his decision: "Not my will, but thine be done" (Luke 22:42). He waited where Judas and the Roman detail could find him, and for horrors to come. That place where he prayed is now marked by a dark church with only a little light filtering in, with an exposed altar that marks the place where he'd sweated so profusely and then said *Yes, I'll go*. I love it that, at the entrance, there is a little sign that says, "No explanations in the church." Its intent is to prevent the tour guides from chattering on—but I love that subtlety that there's no definitive explanation of this mystery that is Jesus and what he embraced in Gethsemane.

An unforgettable moment in that garden outside that church: we'd gathered there for a service of worship and prayer, led by my friend and colleague, Rev. George Ragsdale. As he was reading the story of Jesus's praying there, it began to rain. I was slower than I'd wished to open my umbrella and hold it over George as he continued, undeterred. The pages from which he was reading in his very fine Bible got wet. I apologized later for not protecting it more quickly. But he said he was grateful as, for the rest of his life, when he notices those wrinkly pages, he'll recall being in that place with deep joy.

# The Patron Saint
# of Worried Mothers

When I was little, my family took a vacation through Florida. My sister and I enjoyed St. Augustine: the oldest jail, the Fountain of Youth, Marineland. It's pronounced AuguSTEEN. So imagine my embarrassment during my first week of seminary: I'd read the assignment about the fifth-century person, St. Augustine, raised my hand, called him St. AuguSTEEN, only to be corrected by my professor: "It's AuGUStin."

St. Augustine, born in 354, died in 430, is probably the most important teacher and theologian in all of Christian history. His story, which he shared with us in history's first spiritual autobiography, *The Confessions*, is compelling. Brilliant, but unsettled, he became a great scholar—but hadn't yet converted to Christianity. He fathered a child out of wedlock. Finally, at age thirty-one, he had a profound mystical experience and became a Christian of immense zeal. He was among the first to figure out our theology of the Trinity, of sin and forgiveness, of what to do about Christians and their clergy who caved under pressure and denied Christ—and so much more.

His father was a cruel, cold man, and unfaithful to his wife. But Augustine's mother Monica was tender, holy, and loving. She fretted intensely over her son during his years of troubles and wandering far from God. Once she was praying in church—sobbing actually; Bishop Ambrose saw her, and said, "It's impossible that the son of these tears of yours will perish."[3]

And so she became, not surprisingly, the patron saint of all worried mothers—a huge and holy host. This was dramatized for me the first time I went to Rome. I was eager to see the church called San Agostino (St. Augustine in Italian), not far from the Piazza Navona. Have you noticed huge swaths of stone missing from the Colosseum in Rome? They were repurposed (stolen?) to build this church! St. Augustine isn't buried here, but his mother, St. Monica, is. The sarcophagus bearing her remains is perched up on the wall to the left of the altar.

I entered and thought no one was there. As I approached the altar and looked up to see St. Monica's sarcophagus, I realized I was not alone. My eyes were trying to adjust to the dark, but what I heard was unmistakable: a woman's voice, a tearful, desperate sort of voice. She was repeating over and over and over the same two words: "*Mio bambino, mio bambino, mio bambino.*"

I sat on a wooden bench probably thirty feet behind her, and prayed with her, although she didn't realize I was there. Most certainly, she was a mother, coming to the grave of the patron saint of worried mothers, offering up *mio bambino*, "my child," to God. I had no idea what her *bambino's* trouble was. Fill in the blank. I felt all agony by all parents over all their children over the centuries in her agonized voice in this sacred place.

> *God hears. God's heart breaks.*
> *God loves. God—sometimes?—acts.*
> *And maybe it takes a long time.*

God hears. God's heart breaks. God loves. God—sometimes?—acts. And maybe it takes a long time. Monica prayed intently through a river of tears for many years over her son Augustine. She was merely hoping for his salvation. She could never have anticipated he would one day be deemed a saint—or that she would, too, because of her simple act of praying for him and thus standing in for all of us who've been there, who understand what it is to mutter *Mio bambino, mio bambino, mio bambino*.

I adore Mary Oliver's short poem titled "Don't Worry."

Things take the time they take.
Don't worry.
How many roads did St. Augustine follow
before he became St. Augustine?[4]

Of course, there isn't always a happy ending. But I am moved by Augustine's thoughts when he narrates his mother's death—just weeks after his baptism! "I closed her eyes, and into my heart there flowed together an immense sorrowfulness.... My soul had a deep wound, and my life was as good as dismembered because her life and mine had become one."[5]

Prayer isn't magic. But it does bind us tightly, like twins or like mother and child, to those for whom we pray, and to God. God knows our pains over children who struggle. After all, God watched his own beloved Son suffer such a terrible death on the cross. Prayer is love.

# The Patron Saint of the Pandemic

It's fun bumping into people who are from somewhere or another they think you've not heard of or been to. A cab driver in New York was flummoxed: "You've been to Côte d'Ivoire?" A waiter in Jerusalem was stunned: "You've been to Yerevan?" We all pray to be known, maybe to fit in. Are such surprising moments answered prayers?

An office receptionist's accent prompted me to say, "You're from England?" "Yes." "Where?" "Oh, a little town you've never heard of." "Try me." "It's a couple of hours northeast of London, near the coast." "Yes…?" "Okay, I'm from Norwich." I gleefully said "I've been there! I love Norwich." Flabbergasted, she asked me what on earth had taken me to Norwich.

A few years earlier, I'd taken my oldest child on a driving tour through England to nose out cathedrals, stopping at Lincoln, Durham, Ely, Salisbury, Ripon, Liverpool—and Norwich. This great cathedral features massive, intricate, beautiful cloisters, two stories tall! You can't help but gawk at the spire, 315 feet tall, the second tallest in all of England.

That spire, or rather its predecessor, was blown to the ground by high winds in the year 1362. How staggering was such an event when it befell the citizens of this medieval town, including the woman whom Sarah and I both felt attached to enough to come here in the first place: Julian of Norwich, one of the greatest mystics and theologians of the Middle Ages. She was just twenty years old when that spire tumbled. Everyone must have heard the crash and wept over what must have felt like a sign from God. Not that horrors were new to them: when Julian was just six years old, the bubonic plague (the "Black Death") killed almost half of the city's population.

There's a statue of her in the cathedral. But what we came to Norwich to see was her cell. In her twenties, she moved into a hundred-square-foot cell with three windows and lived inside those walls in seclusion until her death at age seventy-three. She devoted her life to prayer, and providing spiritual counsel to people who would appear at her window—as the plague raged on, and as the Peasants' Revolt took the lives of what few young men remained.

We visited and loved her cell. Mind you, her original cell was bombed and destroyed during World War II. And so, the cell we visited was a reconstruction. This always depresses me a little. But so it is with many historic places we visit. Reconstructions help us envision the original place. Williamsburg is lovely; and although almost none of it is original, you get the feel of the colonial place. Come to think of it, our lives as disciples, and our prayers, are reconstructive; we rebuild now what once was then.

I've dubbed Julian the patron saint of the pandemic. During a long season of plague, she was shut inside a small building. Her message? Or rather, the Message she heard from Jesus when she experienced a series of visions? With steeple stones piled on the ground, and fresh graves outnumbering the old ones, she found intimacy with Jesus as her security: "Thus will I love, and thus do I love, and thus I am safe." "God wants us to know we are equally safe, in woe as in well-being." Julian's most famous words were, "All shall be well, and all shall be well; all manner of things shall be well."[6] This is no sunny optimism about tomorrow being a more chipper day; this is hope, the vested confidence that when all is said and done, the love of God will triumph over plagues, storms, illness, a crumbled Church, political machinations, and even death itself.

# The Cathedral Was for God

April 15, 2019. The phone rang: "Turn on your television." What Ken Follett and his wife saw on the screen when they did was "the wonderful cathedral of Notre-Dame de Paris, one of the greatest achievements of European civilization, on fire. The scene dazed and disturbed us profoundly. I was on the verge of tears."[7] As were we all.

Follett knew before most of the world that the roof would soon collapse—the way engineers knew the Twin Towers would fall when most thought it was just a terrible fire. His novel, *The Pillars of the Earth*, tells of the burning down of a medieval cathedral—so he knew that between the decorative ceiling and the roof were massive wooden (and dried from age) timbers, a tinderbox waiting to ignite.

I want us to visit a few cathedrals together and see what their walls might tell us about prayer. What is a church building if it's not a place, not just to pray, but to teach us how to pray, more expansively, and in communion with others? When I think of any and all those massive churches built centuries before electricity, fuel motors, or steel, centuries before Columbus or Marco Polo, I am in…*awe* is the word, but even *awe* is insufficient. You could stack piles of large churches like the one I serve inside any medieval cathedral. Standing in the plaza in Cologne, you can only gawk at the spire that soars more than 500 feet toward heaven; that's almost two football fields, straight up. Winchester Cathedral has been standing there, two football fields long, for over nine hundred years. The much newer Liverpool Cathedral is even longer. You can barely see the altar from the back. Did John, Paul, George, or Ringo step inside and marvel? Can such places help me develop a sense of stammering awe and reverence before God?

The construction, the quality of the stonework, the intricate wood carvings, the color and images of stained glass filtering the sun's light: people, mere human beings, conceived all this and did this. I cannot think of any human achievement that is as mind-boggling. And the purpose, the motivation, the point of our grandest, most impressive and beautiful accomplishments? Follett's *The Pillars of the Earth* tells us about a mason named Tom:

> He had worked on a cathedral once—Exeter. At first he had treated it like any other job. He had been angry and resentful when the master builder had warned him that his work was not quite up to standard: he knew himself to be rather more careful than the average mason. But then he realized that the walls of a cathedral had to be not just good, but *perfect*. This was because the cathedral was for God, and also because the building was so *big* that the slightest lean in the walls, the merest variation from the absolutely true and level, could weaken the structure fatally. Tom's resentment turned to fascination. The combination of a hugely ambitious building with merciless attention to the smallest detail opened Tom's eyes to the wonder of his craft.[8]

I've tried to imagine what it was like for this mason, or that carpenter, or the grunt guys, or the women who made lunch, or the elderly watching the progress, hoping to stay alive long enough to see their town's new wonder. Did they feel like Tom? How many fell to their deaths or were crushed? I stand, stroll, and sit in cathedrals and ponder their lives—and am moved that this perfect structure in which I'm standing was and is for God. As are our lives. And the whole world. For God.

In Notre-Dame, York Minster, Durham Cathedral, and a few others, I've clambered up into the attics and have discovered elaborate carvings and paintings. Think about it: artists created these unnecessary works of art, knowing they couldn't be seen by worshippers or anybody once the building was finished. Hidden wonders—but not hidden from God. They were crafted only for God's eyes to behold. Like a holy life: it's for God. So how do such marvels inform our prayers in the more average sanctuaries and homes where we find ourselves?

# Praying for the Queen

Not a single medieval cathedral is what today we'd call a "church start." Each one was built over a spot where there had been a church for centuries. Construction began on York Minster in the thirteenth century; but Christians have been in York since the year 180. Think about it: Christianity had spread from a few dozen uneducated individuals without a business plan far away in Palestine all the way to the north of England within a mere 150 years of Jesus's death. And then, after a few centuries, *Voila!* They built an astonishing cathedral.

York Minster is big. It is the largest medieval church in England by volume, with the widest vault and the greatest square footage of stained glass; the great East window is the size of a tennis court. We took our three young children for what proved to be a memorable visit. As we gawked at the place's nooks and crannies and vast expanses of air and light and stone, I learned that Evensong would be happening at 5:30 p.m. I wish I could say my little children were enthralled with the idea of returning for—prayer? and to hear a small choir sing sacred music? But we came. Lots of fidgeting and yawns...

> *Praying isn't just praying your needs.*
> *Prayer is getting caught up*
> *into the needs of God's world.*

But afterwards, they had noticed that we were forced in that service to pray for things we might not normally pray for: the Queen, hunger, peace, the unemployed, the lonely, all prescribed by the *Book of Common Prayer*. A lovely lesson for my kids, and for all of us. Praying isn't just praying your needs. Prayer is getting caught up into the needs of God's world. If you pray in your house, you're unlikely to pray beyond your own needs. But in an unfamiliar church or out in God's world? We'll discover Karl Barth was right: "To clasp the hands in prayer is the beginning of an uprising against the disorder of the world."[9]

# The Labyrinthine Way to Jerusalem

On another family junket, we made it to the cathedral at Chartres. Simon Jenkins calls it "the celebrity capital of the Gothic age."[10] You see it at a great distance, so you can feel like a medieval pilgrim making your way across the meadows. Chartres is impossible not to enjoy—although as we "enjoy" it, I wonder about medieval pilgrims who came there, not as sightseers armed with cameras, but in pursuit of healing from their troubles. Chartres boasted a grand relic: the robe Mary wore when Gabriel announced she would bear God's son. Surely Mary could work a miracle or two for you?

The west façade is clearly the "front," but the north or the south transept would do just fine as the "front" of any other church. The buttresses here are the first I'd spent time with. What a feat of engineering: to realize the weight of high walls, especially with gaps for windows to emit light, could only be sustained by these winged supports, beautiful themselves. Every church has hidden buttresses— not just whatever in the foundations and walls makes the thing stay erect, but spiritual forces, God's firm hand, even if little noticed. The saints of old, who still cluster in and around our buildings that they treasured, buttress us. And I chuckle over Winston Churchill, admitting he wasn't a great churchgoer, claiming to be like those buttresses that support the church, but from the outside.[11]

I love the statues of Old Testament heroes carved above and around Chartres's portals. Just stunning. Abraham, Moses, Samuel, and David not only fulfill an Old Testament-ish function of showing us the way to the climax of God's history with us in Christ; they are among our Communion of Saints, waiting like ushers at the door to greet us and to remind us that what we are about to do in worship isn't some newfangled innovation but is as old as time, trustworthy and enduring.

The beauty of the exterior is exceeded by the glory of the interior. The stained glass creates colorful light amid the darkness. The walls genuinely glow. So much serenity. Robert Barron suggested that the cathedral was "an icon of the sacred, a bearer of the mystery of God."[12] It is, in other words, "an avenue to another world."[13] That avenue, the road you take, is surprisingly in the very floor of Chartres, although most people walk right past—right over it!— without noticing.

Back in the thirteenth century, a labyrinth was cast in limestone into the floor of Chartres Cathedral. It's big, forty feet in diameter.

The word *labyrinth* (outside church) means a complicated, irregular network of passages, a maze, where it's hard to find your way out. I shiver to think of the hedge maze at the Overlook Hotel in *The Shining*...

In Christianity, a labyrinth is a meandering path on a floor or the ground that people take toward a center, a spiritual practice of walking, deliberately, slowly, meditating, praying, and meditating some more. My friend Kathy Mansfield calls it "an embodied prayer," a physical, full-bodied meditation, the gradual movement symbolizing our journey toward our true center, God. Barron writes, "The deepest part of the soul likes to go slow, since it seeks to savor rather than to accomplish; it wants to rest in and contemplate the good rather than to hurry off to another place."[14] In medieval times, people who wished they could make the arduous pilgrimage to Jerusalem but simply could not, due to wars or personal circumstances, found in the labyrinth a thoughtful substitute. Everywhere could be Jerusalem.

So another way to get to Jerusalem right where you find yourself? Some churches and gardens have labyrinths. There are portable labyrinths, but a makeshift labyrinth can easily be created with chalk or a lawnmower! How moving is it that when we trace our steps along a labyrinth, we are united with Christians both now and in the Middle Ages in Chartres—and so many other places around the world!

# Teeming with Life

Solomon's temple was designed, not just to be a spectacular religious building, but to evoke and to give its worshippers a sense of paradise, of natural beauty, of the best of God's marvelous world. So it wasn't just imported, exotic stone, but lots of wood, and decorations that were more green than any other color, suggesting life, growth, flourishing. Even stone breathes and perspires with a kind of living-ness, testifying to God's goodness in creation.

Medieval cathedrals were designed to represent the glories of God's creation indoors. The extraordinary ceiling of Ely Cathedral comes off as a heavenly canopy, drawing our attention and adoration upward. The huge columns inside the Durham Cathedral look like a thick forest of massive trees, each one uniquely crafted, reminding us of the garden of Eden from which humanity had fallen, and the wonderfully restored creation into which we will one day be restored.

Robert Barron describes the goal of these cathedrals, either in the forethought of the architects or just as we experience them today: "to facilitate flight—away from the tiny, cramped room of the ego." To get there, "God's house ought to teem with life. Accordingly, everywhere you turn in a Gothic cathedral, you see, 'carved in the stones and etched in the glass,' God's exuberant creation: vines, leaves, tendrils, trees, birds, fish, dogs."[15] Indeed, what amazes when you visit any and every medieval cathedral is the way the art, the stained glass, the very columns holding up the building, all remind us of the very natural world outside the building.

Church isn't designed to be an alternative to the real world. Worship is a time and space apart from the world in order for us to find our way out into the world. Worship isn't a man-made place distinct from the beauty of the natural world; at its best, church is a place where we realize God's glory in the world we find ourselves in.

The very elements of even an admirable, humanly constructed worship space: it's all God's stuff. The ingenuity to think up sacred space. The wood in the rafters and in the walls, having grown for decades out of God's good earth, finding its ultimate purpose in a space of worship, no less moving than a forest. The stone itself, the most solid conceivable witness to God's ancient creation of the earth, finding its way into the church walls and floor. Indeed, every item in every man-made structure was ultimately crafted by God in creation; all beauty bears witness to God.

Do I find God in a church? or out in nature? Yes. If you ponder this semi-regularly, and keep your eyes peeled for signs of God's presence, surprises await. I recall driving through Provence, and so many roads were lined with those elegant plane trees that arch over the road, as if mimicking what a cathedral does. There's life, and shelter, drawing our attention upward, and forward. My gosh, I'm driving through God's cathedral. In church I hope to sharpen my senses so I can discover the house of God everywhere—in the trees, maybe in the city's tall buildings, down the street—or even in the mirror, as Paul reminds us that "your body is a temple of the Holy Spirit" (1 Corinthians 6:19).

# A Mighty Fortress

The Bible gifts us with fantastic mental images of physical places. As we envision those that are in the Holy Land, we learn how to find holy lands very close to home. In chapter 1 we pondered Psalm 42 and a powerful waterfall at the source of the Jordan—and all our waterfalls. Now, we look to the Psalms for another vivid image of great transport.

"O LORD, you are my shelter and my fortress" (Psalm 91:2, my translation). "The LORD is my rock, and my fortress, ... in whom I take refuge, my ... stronghold" (Psalm 18:2). Many psalms and other passages think of God as a huge, high mountain fortress where you might find shelter and protection from trouble. And a cluster of similar sounding Hebrew words are deployed to depict such places, including *masada*.

Perhaps you have heard of or even visited Masada. Looming above the Dead Sea, miles from civilization in a desolate, rocky region, Masada is a visually stunning rock fortress that rises 1,400 feet above ground level. In the 1960s, Yigael Yadin, a great Israeli military hero, led archaeologists in excavating the lavish palace King Herod built on the top, with Roman baths, and an ingenious aqueduct and cistern system so they would have plenty of water in a place where it rains less than two inches in a year.

The three-tiered palace hangs on the northern face of a massive cliff. How many people died building this should-be Wonder of the World? Today a cable car whisks visitors to the top, although you can walk the snake path, pretty arduous even for the fittest.

What a metaphor for God! Solid, high, impregnable, with caves and niches in which you could hide from predators, enemies, or the brutal sun. And Masada has the inspiring story to complete the image. When the Romans were conquering Judea forty years after Jesus's death, 967 Jewish refugees seized Masada and held out for nearly three years. Masada (or was it their God?) was their fortress, their hiding place.

I wonder if, when we drive the Blue Ridge Parkway and see the Appalachians, or if we're out west marveling at the Rockies—or if you're really lucky and get to visit the Alps or the Andes—instead of just snapping photos for Facebook, or being awestruck by the beauty, grandeur, and sheer scope of such wonders, we might gasp, sigh, and join the psalmist: "The LORD is my rock, and my fortress, ... in whom I take refuge, ... my stronghold" (Psalm 18:2). Moses spent forty days on Mount Sinai. Jesus was transfigured on a mountain. St. Francis loved to climb up high into remote caves above the Rieti Valley, or to his hermitage, *Eremo delle Carceri*, a taxing 3.5-mile hike almost straight uphill from Assisi (which I've walked, but only with my fittest pilgrims!).

Francis studied the fissures, cliffs, and clefts, and thought of God as his rock and fortress—and also of the wounds of Jesus. He believed, as did most medieval people, that when Jesus breathed his last, there was an earthquake in Jerusalem (Matthew 27:51) that rippled all the way to Italy, so every crevice he touched was one more result of Jesus's crucifixion. Also, medieval people pondered the wounds in Jesus's crucified body and thought of them as clefts in the rock, that is, The Rock, Jesus, "Rock of Ages, cleft for me." In the mountains, or any rocky place, simply halt, and ponder "O Lord, you are my shelter and my fortress."

# Of the World, but Not Worldly

A few years ago, I was in Scotland and had planned a day trip with two friends. At breakfast, we announced to our host we were driving down from Edinburgh to Lindisfarne. With her enviable Scottish brogue, she said "Aye, Holy Isle. Have you checked the tide tables?" Tide tables? As it turns out, a narrow spit of land connects Lindisfarne to the mainland. For part of each day, you can drive on it. The rest of the day it's covered by the high tide and you can't get there—or leave. You can't just show up, and you plan your departure time too.

Why did St. Aidan choose such a place for his fledgling Christian community back in the seventh century? Its beauty is captivating, yes. But maybe there was something spiritually profound in the geography of the place, as Magnus Magnusson observed: "It was intimately connected to the mainland, but sufficiently apart from it to encourage a sense of willing withdrawal—it was of the world, but not worldly; insular, but not isolated."[16]

Perhaps this is the ideal for sacred space. Separate, but connected. You plan ahead. Once you're there, you're there. And you're already thinking toward when you're back in the world, to which the church is both intimately connected and yet mystically separate.

Magnusson adds another guess about St. Aidan's motives for settling in such a place: "It must have reminded him of Iona." Iona, the island on the other side of Scotland, was where Aidan had been schooled in the faith. One sacred space elicits memories of another; we sense God here because we sensed God somewhere else, years earlier. The church I'm in today does not much resemble my grandfather's old white A-frame church in the country; but there is a kinship, a family resemblance. It's a church, a sacred space of willing withdrawal, early memories of God renewed, invigorating me as I step forward into the sanctuary now. I'm home, here, but also back there. And then, when I return home, I can be worshipful and very much at home with God.

Lindisfarne suffered terribly at the hands of the terrorist Vikings. The monks who eluded slaughter in 793 fled to Durham. They also managed to hide and spirit away the Lindisfarne Gospels—of stunning beauty. I am moved by the focused care and artistic genius of those monks, so devoted to the stories of Jesus that they tried to mirror the beauty of Jesus in their sacred books to be read in worship and devotion. Lindisfarne is a parable of how the church has always been exposed to peril; and yet our commitment is always to beauty, and we will do whatever to preserve that beauty for future generations.

Iona, by the way, may itself be a different parable of what worship and the Christian life are like. Getting there requires planning, effort, and time; you can't just sashay over to Iona! Once you're in Oban, you drive onto a ferry, which takes you to the Isle of Mull. You drive a narrow, winding road to get to a little foot ferry, which sails the rest of the way to Iona. Worship and the life of faith require some planning, effort, and time. The challenge of the journey is part of the delight and joy. It's not like fast food. It's a feast in the restaurant where advance reservations matter; it's hard to park, and so you linger and relish it once you're there. And you remember.

> *Worship and the life of faith require*
> *some planning, effort, and time.*
> *The challenge of the journey is*
> *part of the delight and joy.*

My friend Kemmer Anderson sent me a postcard with the "Prayer of St. Aidan of Lindisfarne:"

*Leave me alone with God as much as may be.*
*As the tide draws the waters close in upon the shore,*
*Make me an island, set apart,*
*alone with you, God, holy to you.*
*Then with the turning of the tide*
*prepare me to carry your presence to the busy world beyond,*
*the world that rushes in on me*
*till the waters come again and fold me back to you.*

# The Our Father

And finally, prayer happens in a place; but it's always about a person, which we might realize more profoundly when we find that person in a very different place. When the disciples asked Jesus, "Lord, teach us to pray," he answered with what we call "the Lord's Prayer." Short, to the point—and the point wasn't asking God for favors. His prayer—if you pray it very slowly, as I'm sure he did—is more about God than our need, and when it's about us its focus is forgiveness, reconciliation among people, and liberation from evil.

How lovely Jesus opened, not with big fancy descriptives of God (like "almighty, ineffable, Creator of the Universe, stupendous, omnipotent") but with something so simple a child could utter it: *Father. Abba.* Intimate. Relational. Affectionate. Trusting. Jesus as a toddler called Joseph *Abba* as he rested in Joseph's lap, and as he learned carpentry skills. Jesus invites us to call God Abba, Father. It's how to be a child again, the way to vulnerable and beautiful closeness to God who welcomes such closeness. And it implies—doesn't it?—that like Jesus with Joseph, we are apprentices, learning over time the skills in God's mind and heart.

I'll never reflect on "our Father" for long without recalling a magical, holy moment in Kenya. We had gone to visit our ZOE ministry there. For years, Christians built, staffed, and supported orphanages, which housed and fed Kenyan orphans, only to release them at maturity to fend for themselves, likely in immense poverty. ZOE is all about empowerment. Orphans enter the ZOE program, and over time begin to dream of being a hair stylist, a farmer, a furniture builder, a carpenter. They get mentoring from professionals, small business loans, and loads of community, support, and encouragement. By age twenty, most of them are running small businesses and sending their younger siblings to school. A miracle—that really works.

The leader there is one of God's great ones: Reegan Kaberia Mungi. Brilliant and charismatic, he's been offered many profitable posts in business and government. But his calling is to the children, Kenya's orphans. I was with him when he met for the first time with a new class of orphans. Just entering the program, they were all shy, quiet, looking maybe ashamed or lost, always looking down.

Reegan welcomed and embraced each one, and then launched into a sermon. Gradually their faces lifted. A few smiles, then laughter, and tears. The sermon was all Swahili, but you could see him instilling hope and confidence, even God's Holy Spirit, into them. The most moving sermon I've ever witnessed.

Later I asked him what he'd said. "Oh, very simple: I explained to them that God is 'our Father.' Orphans have lost their fathers, and mothers. Without God as their Father, they have no hope. Knowing God as Father, there's nothing they can't do."

"Lord, teach us to pray." We echo the ask of the disciples. Can you make some sort of wall and write on it, or in it? Do you have a kitchen table? Any interesting trees nearby? Who's wailing nearby or in the world? And whom else might you forget in your prayers? What is hidden that God sees? And what's right out in the open that is holy, but you'd missed it?

# CHAPTER 5

# Everywhere Is Nazareth

## *Finding the Way Home*

When I travel, I nose out historic homes of historic people. I love to envision life there back in the day: Monet painting at Giverny, Luther the ex-monk with his noisy family in Wittenberg, Flannery O'Connor on her screened-in porch at Andalusia, Churchill painting at Chartwell, Shakespeare as a wee boy in Stratford-on-Avon, Martin Luther King Jr. sitting with Coretta in the kitchen in Montgomery, or Washington surveying his farm at Mount Vernon—where, today, dressed-up staffers chat with you as if it's 1798. If you ask where Washington is buried, they look puzzled and declare they saw him just a few minutes ago. This time travel, "you are there" feel is what we hope Bible reading will be like!

## At Home in Nazareth

Too bad we can't visit Jesus's childhood home. An intriguing rock-hewn house was found recently that some think might have been his. Regardless, we should picture a small, cramped place, with stone floors and no modern comforts; but of course, all except the wealthiest lived like this during Jesus's time.

Today, Nazareth is a crowded, bustling city; but when Jesus was a child and adolescent, it was an obscure hamlet, population of maybe a hundred. It's fascinating to ponder the fact that Jesus lived for nearly three decades as a regular guy in a regular place, working with Joseph, doing chores around the house (which was probably a single room), chatting with neighbors.[1]

Who knew Jesus was…Jesus? God in the flesh mixed with everybody else in daily life, unnoticed, just another neighbor— perhaps as God is with us in our routines at home, in the yard, down the street, shopping, cooking, working, playing a game, taking a nap. Jesus spent only a couple of years as a miracle worker and dazzling teacher. The vast majority of his time was spent simply being. Being with people in what seemed mundane. God's like that.

Jesus was at home in Nazareth—at least until he served as the Scripture reader one Sabbath and declared Isaiah's prophecy was being fulfilled, like right now, and not to the advantage of his long-time neighbors. The small crowd ushered Jesus out to the precipice that we still visit today: a terrifyingly high cliff where they almost tossed Jesus down to his death (Luke 4:16-30). Jesus was at home, but no longer at home.

St. Francis left his comfortable childhood home in Assisi, where he no longer felt at home, and lived largely out of doors, down in the valley on a pig farm where lepers roamed. With his own hands, using skills he'd honed as a soldier, he rebuilt the little chapel, which today looks like a dollhouse in the middle of the floor of the gigantic basilica, *Santa Maria degli Angeli*, built to protect and showcase that humble stone structure even short people duck to enter. Francis chose to make his home among the poor—to serve them but also to feel closer to Jesus, who relinquished the comforts of heaven to make his home down here among us, and especially among the poor and untouchables.

Carl Sandburg wrote that Abraham Lincoln never felt at home in any one of the thirty-one rooms of the White House. Anne Tyler's novel *Dinner at the Homesick Restaurant* (2011) tells the story of Ezra Tull inheriting Mrs. Scarlatti's restaurant, where he'd worked. He renamed it the Homesick Restaurant. Instead of a menu, you'd name what food you were homesick for, and they'd cook it for you. God seems to have fashioned us with this hankering for home, and yet with gnawing sensation that you're never quite there. You might own and dwell in a fancy house. But "home" is...well, who can say?

St. Augustine was right: "Lord, you have made us for yourself, and our hearts are restless until they find rest in you."[2]...which is why we sing "Softly and tenderly Jesus is calling: Come home," and "When Christ shall come with shout of acclamation and take me home, what joy shall fill my heart." I wonder, in the meantime, if we might learn to reframe our sense of restless dislocation. Instead of fretting over it and trying ever harder to feel at home in the world, we might understand our unease at what God planted in us, sort of a homing device so we will forever seek after God. And then, while we're here, we find new places to be close to God, unexpected, even uncomfortable places—like that pig farm where Francis found a home.

And we can't forget how following God's call can land you far from the home you relinquished to follow. Abraham left Ur for...well, he had no idea where. His tomb in Hebron was 1,200 miles from where he started. Peter finished up in Rome, 2,000 miles from his Capernaum home. Thomas wins the prize though: legend places him 8,000 miles from home, founding churches in India that are still vital today. Instead of spiffing up your home, God might just uproot you to some distant, unforeseen destination.

# My Childhood Home

I've always had this curious itch to drive by and even try to get inside houses where my family used to live. My family lived in Savannah until I was seven years old. I was either proud or puzzled when I drove back into Savannah to conduct a friend's wedding. I'd been away for 32 years, so (still in pre-GPS days), I brought a map—but I didn't need it. I startled myself by driving directly to the little house on Fernwood Drive where we'd lived (it was, of course, littler than I'd remembered), then to Casimir Pulaski Elementary School, and on to Hunter Air Force Base, where my dad was stationed, and where I was born.

How had the map of Howell family places come to be imprinted in my head when I was so young and stay imprinted there for decades? I think of that intriguing verse in Psalm 84: "Blessed are those...in whose heart are the highways to Zion" (v. 5, ESV). Did pilgrims in Bible times remember the route? Or is there some hint that God imprints on our hearts the way to God—so we can find our way home, so we're never too lost?

For my fourth-grade year, my family lived in a trailer out on Wilkinson Boulevard in Charlotte, the city where I live now. That same inner gyroscope tells me "It was right here," even though there are no trailers in sight now. Lisa and I have crept by her childhood home on Macon Avenue near the Grove Park Inn in Asheville. And my own children have detoured through Davidson to find our old parsonage there, with puzzled commentary on what our successors have done with the yard!

Most memorably, I was visiting a friend in Columbia, South Carolina, and took a short detour to 1700 Cofield Drive, home for me from fifth grade until I went off to college, perched on a steep hill that drew a crowd when we got ice or snow. I was one of only two kids I knew who could pedal a bike from bottom to top. In the curve was our house—my parents' "dream house" they'd saved forever to build. Their dream was a bit of a nightmare, as they never declared a cease-fire in the war that was their marriage. Despite the tumult, as a kid I needed a home, and this was it.

I stopped the car, stared, and finally got out to snap a photo with my phone to send to my sister. Then I noticed a woman standing in the door, probably thinking I was a criminal or a weirdo. I waved, and spoke as I walked toward her, telling her my name, and that I'd lived there as a kid. "You're a Howell?" "Yes ma'am." "We bought this house from your folks; been here ever since." Then she made my quirky wish come true: "Would you like to come in?" Would I?

It wasn't much changed, the garage, kitchen, dinette, family room. As I gazed around, and back a few decades, I heard this kindly woman say what I'd heard my own mother say too often: "Why don't you go to your room?"

However, it seemed not to be punitive but inviting—so I made my way down the hall and into what was my room. My host, with stunning graciousness, asked me, "Could I bring you some milk and cookies?" I laughed out loud and embraced her. And then she spoke of her husband, whom I'd hardly noticed as I swooped past the family room, where he was seated, not interacting, leaning against an oxygen tank: "He has congestive heart failure. I believe you're a pastor. Could you pray for him?" And, of course, I did.

Here I was, standing in the home of my troubled but cherished childhood, praying for a man I didn't know, but cared for, not merely because he lived in my home, but because we were connected across time as fellow citizens of a house that was just a house, but not really: it was a home, a place of belonging, not merely to my family or his or theirs, but to God's, even if we only dimly comprehended such things.

> *The good gift of a home, not necessarily the house, yet often in a house, is itself a great grace, stirring an awareness of belonging and safety.*

"Home" is such a prevalent and powerful biblical and theological theme. The good gift of a home, not necessarily the house, yet often in a house, is itself a great grace, stirring an awareness of belonging and safety, even in homes that are less than ideal. Maybe this is the deep reason we pray for and work for those who are homeless, or immigrating, or coping with disaster.

Drive to the Great Smoky Mountains to see what I mean. Dolly Parton, after her song "My Tennessee Mountain Home" became a big hit, built a whole theme park around a replica of her childhood home—which she calls "a golden thread that keeps me tied to eternity."[3] Tourists flock to it by the thousands. They're having fun, but many report being touched by some deep memory and yearning. What's downright shocking is how popular her song is in countries like Kenya, England, and Lebanon, where southern hillbilly culture could not be more alien, and how many visitors to her house are from distant states and nations. Isn't it that home-shaped hole in the heart of every person, God calling to us "softly and tenderly" to "Come home"?

# A Second Home

Sometimes "home" might best be approximated not at our current primary residence, but somewhere else. Jesus had a second home, a house not in Nazareth but in Capernaum. This house we can visit, thanks to a team of archaeologists who uncovered it in the 1960s. Among a warren of interconnected, single and double room small abodes, one house had plastered walls with Christian graffiti—and the remains of a Byzantine church built on top of it. Clearly this was the home of Peter's mother-in-law—the house referred to as "home" every time the Gospels tell us "and Jesus was at home." His home away from home.

You may recall the story in Mark 2: when Jesus was at home, a crowd thronged in to hear him talk. Four guys brought a paralyzed friend on a pallet, but they couldn't get close. So they climbed onto the roof and "dug through." Walls were made of stone, but roofs were thatched, branches and packed dirt. Imagine the debris crashing down on Jesus and those jammed in near him inside! They lowered the paralytic, and Jesus healed him. Why? "He saw their faith." Not the paralytic's faith, but the faith of the four friends! We believe together, and it blesses others.

My truest childhood home, which still lingers in me decades into adulthood, wasn't any of the houses where my nuclear family lived. As a transient Air Force family we moved a lot, and my parents were at war with one another. So my heart's home was my grandparents' home in a sleepy town in the middle of nowhere called Oakboro. My memory of it is expansive, as if it were a huge mansion. As an adult I've visited, and nearly purchased it a couple of times! Just a smallish bungalow, but back then a spacious palace of love, great joy, and belonging.

I've stood in that front yard, under the old oak tree (for which I always assumed the town had been named!), and remembered churning ice cream, playing tag with cousins, and most poignantly, watching my dad and his brothers, all strong, military veterans, weep out loud on one another's shoulders on hearing the news their dad, my Papa Howell, had died. I've even imagined what went on in that yard when my dad returned home from World War II, back in the days of no communication, when so many young boys were killed in action—but then my dad, in his early twenties, being embraced with shouts and tears, probably a lot like the homecoming Jesus pictured when that prodigal finally found his way down the road to home.

I was dumbfounded when I came upon an incandescent moment in Marilynne Robinson's great novel, *Gilead*. When someone dies, we may say "He's gone to a better place." And yet,

> I can't believe that, when we have all been changed and put on incorruptibility, we will forget our fantastic condition of mortality and impermanence, the great bright dream of procreating and perishing that mean the whole world to us. In eternity this world will be Troy, I believe, and all that has passed here will be the epic of the universe, the ballad they sing in the streets. Because I don't imagine any reality putting this one in the shade entirely, and I think piety forbids me to try.[4]

Could it be that the function of a place away from home, a second home, with beloved grandparents, infusing so much grace and shimmering with love and belonging, might be to help us know how to think about a longed-for home, "not made with hands, but eternal in the heavens," so we might believe, and yearn, and even be patient in the waiting? Do we believe in a better place because we've spent time in … a better place?

# Where Did the
# Lord's Supper Happen?

Linger with me in Oakboro for one more recollection. When my sister and I would leave, Papa Howell seemed terribly sad to see us go. So he created this little liturgy of departure: We would be stashed in the car; my dad would back out of the driveway and begin to accelerate toward the town's lone traffic light down the road. As if suddenly remembering what he'd forgotten, Papa Howell would hurry toward the car, imploring us to stop. I would roll down the window, he would reach in his pocket, and press into my palm a fifty-cent piece. In those days, my monthly allowance was fifty cents, so I needed this kind of money—but I never, ever spent a single one of those precious gems.

To this day, when I stand in a line and a priest presses a piece of bread into my hand, I recall the little gifts of Papa Howell. He was giving me money, in a way, but really he was giving himself; he wanted me to be able to clutch a piece of him with me when I was far from him. Maybe in the same way, Jesus knew little pieces of bread could bear the fullness of his entire being and guarantee we'd remember him after he was gone. And dare I ask: was Papa Howell sharing in the Lord's Supper there at the edge of his yard?

We cherish church as home because we share a meal there. And we learn that all meals, just as Bethlehem can show up anywhere, have that sacramental flavor. How many times did we sit down to eat at Mama Howell's small table when a stray cousin or a bricklayer from down the street would materialize? And we knew to wedge him in and share what was passed. Dorothy Day learned about God's grace and how to care for the needy at her table at home: "Let's all try to be poorer. My mother used to say, 'Everyone take less, and there will be room for one more.' There was always room for one more at our table."[5]

I feel sure that Mary's table in Nazareth was such a table. Jesus's second home in Capernaum certainly was. If we have some generous sense of the adjective "sacramental," let's revisit Jerusalem and the place where the sacrament of Holy Communion was birthed. The first time I visited Jerusalem, I followed the signs near the Zion Gate to the Cenacle, the "Upper Room," which looks like the sort of room where we like to think the Last Supper took place.

Fred Craddock, one of our greatest ever teachers of preaching, used to tell the story of his first visit to the Cenacle. His group was waiting at the entrance. Inside was another group led by their pastor, who was saying "This is the very room where Jesus ate the Last Supper with his disciples. You are sitting on the very stone floor around the very table where Jesus broke the bread and shared the cup." He led them in prayer. They were moved to tears.

Then Craddock's group ambled into the room. The tour guide explained, "As you can tell from the ribbed vaults, and the construction of these columns, this room was built twelve or thirteen centuries after the time of Christ. We can't really know where the Last Supper took place." A woman next to Craddock tugged on his sleeve and whispered to him, "I wish I were in that other group."

When I take groups to Israel, I try to explain that Jerusalem is chock full of places pretending to be the real place but are not. Yes, pilgrims have visited and prayed at such places, which gives them their own kind of sacred aura. But what we seek is the real thing, not a fake pretend place that matches up with our fantasies. And there are very real places around Jerusalem and around Galilee where with total confidence we can say Jesus stood here, walked here, prayed here, even died here.

Yet I am not flummoxed in the least that we cannot pinpoint where Jesus shared that Last Supper with his disciples. I'm even appreciative. Why? Wherever it happened in the year 30 CE, I am moved by the mystical miracle that this very meal also happens on Sunday mornings in my sanctuary, in prisons and nursing homes, and has happened in churches where I've worshipped and even preached in Scotland, Lithuania, Kenya, China, Brazil, and all over America—too many to number. Everywhere is that Upper Room.

Or perhaps I should say it's not that the Last Supper happens in all those far-flung locations. Rather, when two or three or a few hundred gather wherever they gather, they are mystically transported to a room in the Middle East and back two thousand years. We are there, and then, with Jesus and the others. Jesus breaks the bread and shares the cup with them, with us. During the pandemic we spoke of virtual worship. Worship is always virtual. We join across space and time and no matter where we are, we find ourselves relocated to the place where Jesus was, and thus still is.

# We Honor God when We Eat

And if this can be so, then so many meals become sacred, pulling the veil off of eternity in surprising ways. Mama Howell's table. Papa Howell's fifty-cent pieces. Back in 1984, I saved up my very limited funds and flew to Rome to see the place, and also to visit my friend Phillip who had gone there to study for the Catholic priesthood. I'd always wanted to see Rome, and getting to visit this greatest of ancient cities in the company of a longtime friend was on the verge of too good to be true.

We meandered together around St. Peter's Basilica, *San Pietro in Vincoli*, and other great churches—and quite a few that are obscure, hard to find, unheard of, and wonderful. We took the train to Assisi for several days, the beginnings of my lifelong (now!) obsession with St. Francis.

Neither of us had much money, so generally we ate with the other Catholic monks and students with whom he lived at the American University in Rome. But we took two nights out on the town and found our way to two of his favorite restaurants: *Da Pancrazio*, just off the *Campo de Fiori*, built over the ruins (still visible in the basement!) of Pompey's theater, where Julius Caesar was assassinated; and another night at *Il Buco*, a tiny restaurant not far from the Pantheon, but not named by Rick Steves or Fodor's—so it's very Roman, with precious few Americans.

People who know I've been to Rome often will ask "Do you have a restaurant recommendation in Rome?" I always respond, "Yes, walk into any restaurant, it will amaze you." And yet I do urge folks to find *Da Pancrazio* and *Il Buco*. Yes, it's elitist to have something so grandiose as "my favorite restaurants in Rome." But they are favorites, not because I'm sure their cuisine or service is superior, but because I have history there. Every time I am back in Rome (and I'm very lucky to have been back quite a few times, even for a couple of meetings!), I drag whoever is with me there.

Familiarity? Yes, a comforting, homey thing. But when I sit on the patio over a long leisurely dinner at *Da Pancrazio*, I reminisce about prior visits, and other people with whom I've broken bread and devoured pasta in that very spot. When I walk into *Il Buco*, and discover to my amazement that Franco, the very waiter who served Philip and me in 1984, is still working there three decades later, and is still charming and efficient (and always pretends he remembers me well and that we are great friends!), I feel entirely at home—on the other side of the globe.

If these illustrations are too hifalutin, think with me of diners and burger joints that are known far and wide and function as pilgrimage destinations, perhaps where you ate in college and still do as an alumnus decades later—or iconic, must-visit spots like Café du Monde in New Orleans, Katz's Deli in Manhattan, or the Bluebird Café in Nashville. Or just that hole-in-the-wall you and yours know and love.

> *Clearly, God made food, and eating together, a way, maybe the best way, to find God and one another.*

Clearly, God made food, and eating together, a way, maybe the best way, to find God and one another. Ellen Davis, pondering the details in the days of creation of all the plants and animals in Genesis 1, suggests that God is "stocking the pantry." Indeed, "Eating is at the heart of our relationship with God and all that God has made. . . . Eating is practical theology—it gives the opportunity to honor God with our bodies. Our never-failing hunger is a steady reminder to acknowledge God."[6] Or as my friend Leighton Ford put it, after viewing what makes me apoplectic when watching my alleged squirrel-proof bird feeder: "I am watching birds pecking on the feeder and one lone acrobatic squirrel twisting himself in every direction hoping for just a taste of the good stuff; if only my soul was so persistent and hungry as your other creatures."

And we are hungry to be with other creatures, friends, family, people who could be friends if we'd eat with them. Fights can erupt at the dinner table, but far more likely we'll find peace and love. You have to share; you pass the potatoes and don't greedily grab the last biscuit. You wait until others have eaten, even if they are slow and you're a gobbler. You help clean up. It's community—which is what God made us for, and what heaven will be like. All the Bible's images of heaven envision it as a lavish feast where nobody eats alone.

Jesus loved food. He was always eating with other people, even the unlikely people. He cooked; did he learn this from his mother? And he made a meal into his best illustration of all he was about. That community is never just the people we like, or the people like us. By the virtuality of Jesus's presence, and then in every meal in every place, we discern what we would otherwise miss: the joy, the fellowship, and of course, new aches and a lot of rethinking. Come with me on an excursion to China and to east Africa before we finish up at the homes of our personal ancestors.

# Nothing Can Separate Us

In 1985 I joined a small group travelling to Fuzhou, a mid-sized city by China's standards, with my ethics professor at Duke, Creighton Lacy—to his childhood home. He'd grown up there in a missionary family. But in 1948, Mao Zedong's regime expelled them from the country—all except for Lacy's father, who had served as the Methodist bishop of Fuzhou. Thirty-seven years later, Lacy could only speculate what his father's fate had been.

After dinner one evening, a man Lacy recalled from childhood came by the hotel and told us his and Bishop Lacy's story. They had been imprisoned together and treated cruelly. The bishop fell ill, but no doctor was summoned. And so he'd died there, in his friend's arms. On hearing this, all we could do was sit with our heads hung in a long, numb silence.

The next evening after we learned this awful truth, we and our hosts worshipped together. I was thunderstruck as I watched Lacy reading in English, and his and his father's friend translating into Chinese, words from another prisoner, Paul, which will forever resonate differently in me:

> *If God is for us, who is against us? ... Who shall bring any charge against God's elect? ... Who shall separate us from the love of Christ? Shall tribulation, or distress, or persecution, or famine, or nakedness, or peril, or sword? As it is written,*
>
> > *"For thy sake we are being killed all the day long;*
> > *we are regarded as sheep to be slaughtered."*
>
> *No, in all these things we are more than conquerors through him who loved us. For I am sure that neither death, nor life, nor angels, nor principalities, nor things present, nor things to come, nor powers, nor height, nor depth, nor anything else in all creation, will be able to separate us from the love of God in Christ Jesus our Lord.*
>
> (Romans 8:31-39)

Some funny things happened on that trip. I discovered that Chinese food—that is, the food the Chinese actually eat day by day, the food served in their restaurants—is entirely different from the fare you find in America's Chinese restaurants. We were treated to hundred-year eggs, octopus, and some simply unidentifiable dishes—and chopsticks weren't optional. In one rural home, the mom served us a lunch of shelled peanuts and rice. She kindly refrained from laughing as I poked at and chased the slippery peanuts and flaky rice around my plate.

One woman in our group had blonde hair. In less urban places, bystanders would gawk, ask for photos, and even reach out to touch this novelty they'd not seen, as China had only recently opened up to travelers from places like America.

A visit to a school and then a church next door revealed more about our unconsidered biases than their customs. The first classroom had a map of the world on the wall. My friend pointed at it and in a harrumph said (and I'm not making this up) "Look! How terrible that they have China in the middle of this map! Everybody knows America is in the center." I couldn't, and still can't muster any rational response to this.

And then we entered the church. In China, churches were abolished for decades, but by 1985 they were popping up here and there. The one we visited had been a church back in the day. The Communists morphed it into a factory. Now it had been reclaimed as a church. Oddly, during the years China welcomed American missionaries into their country, Christianity grew a little bit, not a lot. Once the missionaries were thrown out, and Christianity was suppressed, the church—with no buildings, and only in secret— grew far more rapidly than when it had been legal. When you stand in a church in China and hear this narrative of clandestine gatherings and smuggled Bibles, you shudder when you think how lackadaisical American Christians can be, picky about preachers or music, missing worship to go fishing or to sleep in, their Bibles lonely from neglect.

And then there was the flag. The church sanctuary was modestly appointed, with folding chairs, a simple wooden cross behind a rostrum. Just outside the window to the left was a pole flying the national flag of China. Several in our group were mortified by this, declaring things like "I can't believe they have such a flag so close to the church—and visible from inside!" I could only counter (and I hope I was gentle) that many churches in America have the stars and stripes, not just near the building, but up front, at the very altar. One man told me "That's different."

# Put Away the Gods
# Your Fathers Served

So, "home" has its treasures and joys, even in the thick of longing and loss. There also can be a kind of hidden peril in places that feel like home, and even with the remarkable, lovely people who made the house a home for us. I wonder about Dolly Parton's parents in her Tennessee mountain home, or—and I get the shivers even letting my mind my wander toward the mere suggestion—my own grandparents. I adore them, and owe them my life and every sense of goodness, resilience, and hope that are woven into the fiber of my being. My grandparents were deeply committed Christians. I possess clear evidence in their badly worn, well-marked Bibles and memories of them singing hymns while going about their chores and kneeling with me and my cousins morning and evening. But what were their blind spots?

They, and Dolly's parents, were white Southerners during Jim Crow. It's foolish to judge people of prior eras by modern progressive standards. And yet, to reckon with what's in the soil of "home," and what's in our spiritual DNA may be a big piece of the puzzle in our own quest to find our way home to our true selves, and to God. Isabel Wilkerson reminds us that when you go to the doctor, they hand you that clipboard that asks if you've had diabetes or heart issues in your family, extending back a couple of generations. No shaming if you check a box. But the doctor needs to know what's rattling around in you to treat you properly today.[7] Same for our spiritual journey.

How often does the Bible itself urge keeping some distance from our beloved ancestors and their cherished but flawed beliefs? Joshua, thirty seconds before his glorious declaration that "as for me and my house, we will serve the Lord" (Joshua 24:15) invites the Israelites to "put away the gods which your fathers served beyond the River" (Joshua 24:14). Could it be our journey involves finding a new space, different from, and closer to the truth than the spirituality of our parents, even the most beloved? They may have instilled in us the very faith we have to ask such a question! Or perhaps, as Jonathan Sacks suggested, our parents may have been on their own journey to a new space that was truer than that of *their* parents.[8] God called Abraham away from the idols of Ur; but his father Terah went with him, at least halfway to Haran (Genesis 11:31).

> *Could it be our journey involves finding a new space, different from, and closer to the truth than the spirituality of our parents, even the most beloved?*

As a grown-up, I travelled with my wife and three children to visit two spots just outside Savannah, Georgia, places that rank high for me among my happiest childhood memories. Both were Civil War forts. Fort Pulaski, a massive brick fortress built in 1829 on Cockspur Island, the chief engineer being none other than Robert E. Lee, who'd just graduated from West Point; and Fort McAllister, less impressive but more natural earthwork fortifications, with underground tunnels. Why did I love these places, which my family frequented? Did the idea of soldiers doing battle fire my imagination, surveying the cannons, the little slits for riflemen, a drawbridge over a moat? Or were our picnics and exploring the happy days for my family, which struggled to find harmony at home?

If you're a Southerner, and probably if you're from anywhere at all, there's always some awful ambiguity to the places you enjoy. Monticello, Jefferson's marvelous house, functioned on the backs of slaves, including some parented by Jefferson himself. Internationally: we admire St. Peter's, the splendid basilica in Rome, but learn it was built with funds swindled from impoverished peasants duped into thinking they were getting their loved ones' souls out of Purgatory.

Fort Pulaski was pounded into submission, the walls still bearing the pockmarks of the northern bombardment, defending the Rebel cause, the institution of slavery—and the same for Fort McAllister. We loved frolicking around the earthworks in the shade of moss-draped trees; but when it was time to leave, the gift shop featured nothing but items bearing the Confederate flag.

What is the thoughtful Christian, yearning to be holy, to do? Avoid Fort Pulaski or St. Peter's in Rome? Or do we explain away the ugliness? Back then, people didn't know better, right? I wonder if the hard realities of such places—and they are everywhere!—are mirror images of you and me, beautiful, made in God's image, temples of the Holy Spirit, and yet so very broken, sinful, confused, even addicted to what is not of God and not healthy for our spiritual selves. And aren't such places the kind of places such beautiful and broken people are bound to produce?

We must be able to live with such awful ambiguity because God made us this way, and Jesus himself came to bear that ambiguity. It's as if we are our own reminders that there is so much good, and yet so much trouble, glorious wonder, and embarrassing stupidity—and hence our deep, constant need for God's mercy, and God's healing power, even as we delight in God's gifts and blessings. God really has imprinted into us the recognition of our need, which is itself the way home.

# Finding the Other Descendants

Lots of people get interested in their ancestry. Online you can plunge into bottomless rabbit holes of information from census and burial records; and you can prick your finger and learn about your bloodlines. But my wife, Lisa, got intrigued by the question of not merely who her ancestors were, but, Did they own slaves? And if so, Who were they? And Who were their descendants? So we've poked around in quite a few cemeteries and have cleared debris from the graves of a couple of grandchildren of former family slaves. Our dream is to come face-to-face one day with a living descendant, although we haven't devised a plan about what to do should we succeed.

So come with me to one of America's loveliest college towns: Princeton, New Jersey. For several years I had a biannual meeting here. When those meetings would get a little dull, I'd stare out the window. I noticed an old, fabulous mansion across the street. On our lunch break one day, I walked across and discovered it was Morven, once the residence of the governors of New Jersey, but originally the home of Richard Stockton, signer of the Declaration of Independence, and many of his descendants.

Now, my wife, Lisa, was (is!) a Stockton. And she's kin: her great-great-great-great-great-grandfather was Richard's uncle. Lots of Stocktons in this clan have had amazing careers in government, law, and the church. So I finally took her for her first visit to Morven, a mansion that is beautifully cared for with historic exhibits. The curator even gave us a personal tour. I love that title, "curator." We are all of us called to be curators, custodians, and carers for our past, the great people and stories and the sorry messes too. Our past really is...us. The genes, the stories, all we inherit, lovely and embarrassing.

Of course, I had to take her to the cemeteries. Richard the Signer was buried at the Stony Brook Meeting House. Small and rustic, this cemetery, has old, worn, illegible stubs of stones scattered across a grassy square. But as a lifelong obsessive when it comes to cemeteries, when I visited the larger Princeton Cemetery, I felt as if I'd died and gone to heaven (figuratively, of course!). President Grover Cleveland, Aaron Burr, Kurt Gödel, Paul Tulane, George Gallup, and a relative unknown: the first African American student and graduate of Princeton public schools, who went on to study in Paris and became a successful businesswoman named Christine Howell. And a host of great theologians, including Jonathan Edwards (who sparked America's "Great Awakening" in the eighteenth century), and Bruce Metzger (lead translator of the Revised Standard Version).

As believers, we are always indebted to great believers and thinkers who've gone before us. I love the old story (maybe apocryphal) about Lyndon Baines Johnson, when he first ran for the Senate, with some of his henchmen scouring a cemetery with flashlights fraudulently registering voters. A guy skipped one headstone, as it was hard to read, but LBJ insisted he go back: "He has as much of a right to vote as anybody else in this cemetery!"[9] I always think the citizens of the cemeteries have maybe a better right to vote on the things that matter—if we can listen to them.

We lingered over the grave of Robert F. Stockton, the "Commodore," Richard the Signer's grandson, who negotiated the treaty to create the nation of Liberia. When I preached in Liberia, I told the crowd of my personal connection. They stood and cheered!—but good grief, the Commodore's intentions were to get rid of the black people nobody in America wanted.

We all of us are mixed bags morally and spiritually. Morven House features, although not in a belligerent, in-your-face guilt-inducing way, the slaves the family held, the laborers who made life in such a mansion easy and delightful for Richard and the Commodore and the rest of them. Those Stocktons were fine people of grand achievements—and yet with terrible blind spots. I wonder what mine are. We pray that God will shine some flashlight on ours, so we might be a bit more holy, a little less foolish, and more of a blessing to others.

# Wherever I Am

So, we've visited quite a few houses and restaurants and cemeteries in this quest for home. When you read the word *home*, what place comes to mind? Do you feel a warm coziness? Or do you tense up a little? Does no single place register in you? Do you have a sense of being at home where you live right now?

> *In this life we never feel entirely at home. God created in us that insatiable yearning to be at home with God, and the rest of the saints in glory.*

The Bible speaks so often of the notion of our home being with God. Thomas Merton, in a prayer, said "Let this be my only consolation, that wherever I am You, my Lord, are loved.[10] Can we manage to conceive that wherever we are, there we are loved, and God is loved—and that is then home? Yes, there's that inevitable restlessness we feel—that God made us to feel—so that in this life we never feel entirely at home. God created in us that insatiable yearning to be at home with God, and the rest of the saints in glory.

But in the meantime, aren't there hints and manifestations of that ultimate home? If you are blessed with a lovely, supportive family, and maybe especially if you have a house, a home where everyone knows the nooks and crannies well from years of occupying the place, you get some good glimpses. For others it may be more momentary. A satisfying meal with somebody who cares. A listening ear prompting you to say more than you'd intended. A tender embrace.

Maybe our home with God is like a mobile home, or an RV. You're on the road—again. But then you park somewhere for a while. And then you're moving once more. Jesus had nowhere to lay his head, so he was always on the move. Yet his clear destination always was Jerusalem, where he was most at home enduring hostility and bearing pain so the rest of us would know the way home.

# CHAPTER 6

# Everywhere Is Jerusalem

## *Places of Sorrow and Hope*

When my mother died in 2019, Lisa and I took the urn with her cremains to the Rose Hill Cemetery in York, South Carolina, where she still rests next to her Momma and Father (which is what she called them, revealing precisely how she felt about both of them). A couple of blocks before we got there, I noticed a man with a reflective vest trudging along the street—and he was hauling a large cross! I was confused, as it was Ash Wednesday, not Good Friday.

I thought of Tom in Pat Conroy's *The Prince of Tides*, who confessed "I grew up loathing Good Fridays" due to his grandfather's "overenthusiastic commemoration of Christ's passion," which was hauling a ninety-pound wooden cross he'd made through the streets of Colleton. Although Tom saw some "lunatic beauty" in this, he "would have preferred" something quieter, "more contemplative....It embarrassed me deeply." Humorously, once his grandfather was older, he had to attach a little squeaky wheel...and also funny in a different way was that "my grandmother expressed her own mortification by retreating to her bedroom with a full bottle of Beefeater gin.... When [his] walk was completed,... so was the bottle."[1]

# Maundy Thursday Late

On *the* Good Friday, Jesus carried the cross on which he would be nailed until he couldn't. My pilgrim groups walk the historic *Via Dolorosa* in Jerusalem, tracking Jesus's path from his bogus trial to Calvary. I pause, shudder, sigh, and nod when I think of the millions of pilgrims over the centuries who made long, arduous journeys to walk this *Via Dolorosa*, their feet on sacred pavements, their muscles moving along the way where Jesus made an even longer journey. Sure, the route probably isn't historically exact. But didn't Jesus go sorrowing and bearing his cross all over the place? Doesn't he ask us to do the same?

There's an unexpected turn in the path where Simon of Cyrene picked up that cross—where I always worry I'll lose a few stragglers. By that time, it was too late for Jesus. The real drama, the irrevocable decision that he made (and it's important to note it was his call, not Judas's or Pilate's) came the night before in the garden of Gethsemane. Maundy Thursday is for us the evening we mark Jesus's Last Supper, and rightly so. But when that dinner was over, he walked out onto the streets of the city, down through the Kidron Valley, and into a little grove of olive trees. Did Jesus weigh the shape of those trees in the shadows? Ancient, these trees, gnarled, looking old and weary. Jesus must have thought *These trees, my friends, feel like I do*.

His groans were audible. His perspiration got compared to droplets of blood, as if in grievous anticipation of what would come in just a few hours. With immense courage and faith, Jesus offered himself to God his Father. No passive acquiescence to fate, but a bold decision to bear God's love into the grinder of those who insist that force is the only way. When Judas, one of his dearest friends, arrived at the head of a band of soldiers, Jesus was neither angry nor even disturbed. He loved, calling him "friend."

He was calm facing the heavily armed squadron sent to haul him off. I love the unexplained detail recorded only in John 18:6. Responding to their declaration they'd come for "Jesus of Nazareth," he said simply "I am he." Their response? They "fell to the ground." That's what the disciples had done at the Transfiguration. That's what Moses did at the burning bush when God said, "I AM WHO I AM." Jesus is no danger to them. It's as if their legs just give way in the face of so much love, so much holiness, so much courage. When I visit Gethsemane, I try to visualize these things. I am in awe once again in this place of sorrow, marked by the sorrowing trees.

# Sacred Places of Sorrow

There's probably a spectrum of people when it comes to being eager to visit places that mark sorrow. I'm on the high end of those who dig visiting cemeteries. Often memorials to loss have a haunting beauty and dignity: Arlington National Cemetery; the cemetery for World War II Allied soldiers in the valley just below Assisi, the home of history's greatest ambassador for peace; the hillside cemetery filled with primarily young soldiers from Australia, killed so far from home from the battle of Gallipoli in World War I; our church's columbarium.

Some are personal, like that turn no one else notices on Highway 24 where a driver crossed the center line and cost my grandfather his life. Some cemeteries are only now being discovered. Black cemeteries, hidden away and neglected by municipalities, witness to Greg Melville's wry observation: "Our cemeteries reveal where our values lie and how we lie about our values."[2] My wife has rounded up quite a few of us to hack away at the overgrowth at the Odd Fellows Cemetery in Winston-Salem, where her sleuthing has identified the graves of descendants of slaves her ancestors owned. A place of sorrow, with an implied moral imperative.

Some places of sorrow are architectural marvels, and all you can do is shudder over the evil they commemorate. When we visit one of our mission partners (Project AGAPE), we take time at the Armenian Genocide Memorial in Yerevan, where 1.5 million were slaughtered by the Ottoman Turks. The Memorial is in the shadow of Mount Ararat, where God promised not to wipe us off the earth for our bad behavior—which I suppose is the only reason we're still here. A display there reminds us of Hitler's cynical remark when he instigated the Holocaust: "Who, after all, speaks today of the annihilation of the Armenians?"[3]

...which takes us to the world's most important (and best) Holocaust memorial: Yad Vashem, on the outskirts of Jerusalem, its displays unmatched in quality, quantity, and depth. Beyond the main building, you can walk through The Valley of the Communities, set in stone like a massive map of Europe, showing whole cities whose Jewish populations were entirely wiped out by the end of World War II—many of which you and I have visited. The Garden of the Righteous Among the Nations features trees planted to honor Gentiles who sheltered Jews, including Corrie ten Boom, Oskar Schindler, and quite a few Armenians and Ukrainians.

Most beautiful, haunting, numbing, and elegant is the Children's Memorial, a warren of mirrors with the flickering light of just five candles creating a galaxy effect in the dark. The names of the 1.5 million children killed by the Nazis are read continuously.

It takes three months to read all the names. You leave feeling overwhelmed, numb, shaken by what you already knew. You shudder, as the number of violent killings of children that should appall us is exactly one. And then another one.

A newer marker of evil and sorrow is the National Memorial for Peace and Justice in Alabama. The design and landscaping are admirable, its sculptures lifelike and agonizing. Some eight hundred steel monoliths hang from the ceiling, one for each county in the U.S. where lynchings took place. The names of the victims are engraved. It's more than you can fathom or absorb. I had the painful privilege of walking among them with my friend Richard Harrison, who wept as he pointed to three names of his own kinfolk. This isn't ancient history. Quite a few of those lynchings happened in my lifetime.

Eddie Glaude reflects on how this memorial disrupts what we hope to find in memorials, like "a triumphalist story of redemption," or a "story of moral courage."[4] Instead, we find mute witnesses to how horrible humanity has been, and can be. It's a warning, of course. And an indictment. James Cone's *The Cross and the Lynching Tree* makes me shiver, as he names how supposedly Christian churches were complicit and even instigators in such horrors.

But without shutting down the implicit demand for change on race today, there's also something sacred about the Memorial. Only God can make a hall of shame sacred. What else was God's intent in making the axis of our salvation the grotesque, unjust execution of a pure, innocent man, hung up to die while being mocked?

And far too young. Of course, every person you love dies too young. To draw close to the heart of God, we are to be attentive to death—honorable, courageous deaths; unjust, criminal deaths; natural deaths; and sudden deaths. And our spiritual journey is itself a journey toward death. We grow as we ponder the place where evil will be no more, where every tear will be wiped away. We ponder our mortality, the brevity of time that is ours, that this world isn't all there is.

> *We grow as we ponder the place where evil will be no more, where every tear will be wiped away. We ponder our mortality, the brevity of time that is ours, that this world isn't all there is.*

But then, gosh, while we're still here, we get busy heeding words like those of Maya Angelou at the Legacy Museum in Montgomery: "History, despite its wrenching pain, cannot be unlived, but if faced with courage, need not be lived again." Next time a Hitler says "Who cares?" we'll say "We do."

# Not "On a Hill Far Away"

So in these sorrowful spaces, which nonetheless are sacred, we begin to see how Calvary isn't just in the Holy Land, but, hauntingly, everywhere. One of the big surprises for pilgrims as we find our way around in Jerusalem is when we arrive at the place where Jesus was crucified. We might sing "On a hill far away...," but the spot where Jesus was crucified is now at the top of a staircase beneath a fairly gaudy, even kitschy altar in a crowded building. And then the place where Jesus was buried? It's in the same gaudy, crowded building.

When Helen, the mother of the emperor Constantine, arrived in Palestine, she asked where these most glorious events had happened. And then she did what pious Christians with great resources have always done at sacred places: she built a big church on top of it, and in this case, both the place of execution and burial, which were not far apart. The Church of the Holy Sepulchre has stood ever since as the most sacred site in Christendom, despite earthquakes, invasions, fires, and rebuilding projects.

You enter the church through massive wooden doors and immediately turn to the right to scale the steps to Calvary. There can be pushing, shoving, and cutting in line, and the press of the crowd leaves you little time to say your prayers at the altar. Somehow, for me, the chaos is just right. What if few or no one came? And at the real Crucifixion, there was traffic on the road and considerable confusion.

After your less-than-serene stop at Calvary, you descend the staircase to a long stone slab: the Stone of Unction, where Jesus's body was laid in preparation for burial. Women kneel, kiss the stone, and rub it with their kerchiefs as candlelit lanterns hover overhead. Lovely, as if the stone slab invites and ennobles our own grief over Jesus, and all the others too.

Then you make your way to a much longer line, where people wait for hours to step briefly inside Jesus's tomb. It doesn't look like a tomb and hasn't since Helen's day. The stone on which Jesus was stretched at sundown on Good Friday was built into an altar— and after many reconstructions, it's still there, inside a little church building in the middle of the floor of the larger church building. The Edicule fields thousands daily for just a sneak peek inside— which, if you think about it, was all the women and the disciples had on Easter morning! In 2016-17, *National Geographic* covered the stunning restoration of the Edicule, which was on the verge of catastrophic collapse; and their published report in their magazine and online provides us with the first photos of the interior of what was the tomb, unseen for centuries.

I'm sure many of us would prefer that idea of a "hill faraway" out in open country, or a cave tomb that still looks like a cave bordered by a garden. It can be disillusioning to battle a crowd, the racket, the long line—not to mention learning about the ferocious territorial battles vying Christian groups have engaged in over the place. And yet, this was the kind of world Jesus came to save. This is the real world in which we live with and for Jesus, or not at all.

The incandescent power of the way God made this place of sorrow and shame sacred manifests itself in the way, clearly, Everywhere is Calvary: crucifixes looming above church altars, above the bed at home, on a chain around your neck, crosses affixed atop churches and cemetery markers. So easily trivialized; and yet, even if we hurry on past the Calvaries we encounter, the sorrowing Jesus, bearing and ennobling the shame, is right there, all the time.

# Underground Portals to Heaven

And so we begin to explore places where sorrow and shame are yanked toward hope. If I say "catacombs," most people think of Rome, although Paris, London, Palermo, and other cities have them. The most visited catacombs, and the most famous, are on the Appian Way outside Rome. I've been there, but I much prefer the catacombs of Priscilla. Fewer buses, rarely a crowd, a thicket of tombs to inspect, and tantalizing art.

What are catacombs? Underground passages, carved out by human beings, not nature, utilized to bury the dead, typically in shelf-like niches cut out into the walls. Many are decorated with religious symbols, artwork, and carvings—and they were much favored by the early Christians.

In ancient Rome, burials had to be outside the city walls. The whole specter of death was antithetical to the business and pleasure life of the city! And Roman tombs frequently had cynical epitaphs—including the popular "I wasn't, I was, I am not, I do not care." Christians cared, and believed they not only were, but continued in eternal life with God and others.

Instead of avoiding burial places, Christians got as close to them as possible. They worshipped and prayed at tombs—and in the catacombs. Why? A tomb, for them, was like a portal through which one travelled to the direct presence of God. To touch a tomb was to touch the door where God and the saints were just on the other side. Death became a friend, not a dreaded foe. Mortality was the truth about reality and need not be feared or denied.

And so Christians gathered in the cool shelter of the catacombs—for prayers, services, and meals. The painted decorations in Priscilla are striking—not designed to be pretty so much as to evoke hope and eternity. Biblical scenes that dreamed of life beyond suffering and death were graphically depicted: Jonah coming out of the whale's mouth. Daniel safe in the lion's den. Lazarus emerging from the grave. Shadrach, Meshach, and Abednego in the fiery furnace. Noah surviving the flood. Visitors gazed at these simple images by candlelight and were filled with hope—for those they'd loved and lost, and for themselves.

Of course, there were wall paintings of Jesus and the disciples, and holy men and women. Jesus eating with his disciples, at the Last Supper or other meals, must have had a powerful impact on those who had brought picnic baskets to dine on spread-out blankets near the graves of those whom they believed were right then and there with Jesus. In the Priscilla catacombs gift shop, I purchased a ceramic copy of Jesus and friends at table—and it's fixed above the door of the entrance to our dining room at home. I'm 4,800 miles from Priscilla, which is two thousand miles from Jerusalem, and we're all about two thousand years from the time of Jesus, and who knows how far from heaven—and yet, mystically, miraculously, and wonderfully, we are very close.

# You Never Stop Being Loved

My mind meanders through so many memories of cemeteries and graves and columbariums where I have visited and prayed. Naturally, I think of the Oakboro cemetery where my grandparents, aunts, and uncles are buried. In the crypt of the basilica of St. Francis, you can kneel or sit on small wooden benches before Francis's tomb, which is surrounded, as he was in life, not by his family but by his closest friends, his spiritual family. As a kid, I was obsessed with John F. Kennedy, his sudden assassination, and that eternal flame over his grave in Arlington; the first time I visited as an adult, I knelt and . . . well, I'm not sure what I was thinking or feeling.

I knelt at the grave of C. S. Lewis and thanked God for inspiring such witty and persuasive apologetic writings, and not far from there I knelt at the grave of his close friend J. R. R. Tolkien, and thanked God for whatever divine muse plunked the notion of Middle Earth, hobbits, dwarves, elves, and ents into his head. And after many trips to Israel, I stood with my friend Rabbi Murray Ezring before the elegant, simple tombstone of Yitzhak Rabin, whom I count as the greatest Israeli leader, whose shocking assassination in 1995 still makes me shudder. He was the best chance ever at peace, snuffed out by a crazed assassin's bullet. His tombstone simply says, "Yitzhak Rabin." Enough said. I sighed and had a few tears.

In her charming novel, *Animal Dreams*, Barbara Kingsolver tells about the town of Grace, where every year they celebrate the "Day of the Dead." The citizens go out to the cemetery and decorate the tombs, strewing flowers all over the ground; they share a festive meal, children run and play and sing among the graves, all of this done with loving care. Kingsolver concluded: "It was a comfort to see this attention lavished on the dead. In these families you would never stop being loved."[5]

# Peter Is Here

When people visit Rome, they make sure they get to the Colosseum, the Spanish Steps, Trevi Fountain, the Piazza Navona, Sistine Chapel, and of course St. Peter's Basilica. Yet, when people ask me, I tell them, "Don't miss what's underneath St. Peter's." Not just the crypt, which is easily visitable, but underneath the crypt. It's almost a parable of the Christian life: the real story, the greatest beauty, isn't obvious, easy, or on the surface of things, but deeper, hidden away, accessible but not easily accessible.

So what could conceivably be under the crypt, which is usually the very basement of a church? The St. Peter's we know was built in the sixteenth century. It took a century to complete; its architects included Michelangelo, Raphael, and Bernini. And sadly, most of the funding came from the corrupt sale of indulgences all across Europe—the venal practice that prompted the Protestant Reformation! It's always this way: Christendom's grandest church paid for by swindlers, like the Colosseum funded by treasures pilfered from the Jerusalem temple.

But there was an older, original St. Peter's, built in the fourth century by the emperor Constantine. The site he chose? Obviously, the tomb of St. Peter. Jesus had said of Peter, "On this rock I will build my church" (Matthew 16:18). So, beginning in the 1940s, archaeologists dug under the St. Peter's we know, and through the debris left from its predecessor. They discovered a necropolis (literally a "city of the dead," really just a cemetery) dating to New Testament times. It wasn't a catacomb, but an open-air cemetery.

There were dozens of mausoleums, many of their occupants being wealthy, given the mosaics, frescos, and ornate carvings. Amazing. All of this was opened up, and now, deep underground, you can walk what once were the streets of a massive cemetery.

You have to apply ahead of time for tickets from the Vatican, as the number of visitors is strictly limited. Guides walk you through it all to its climax, a grave with a faded inscription that declares "Peter is here." They found traces of veneration and what may have been an ancient altar dating to shortly after Peter's death. It's chilling, thrilling—and even if you scratch your cynical head (like I do) and puzzle over if this is really the place, the evidence is pretty darn good. The Vatican website provides a 360° virtual tour, challenging to navigate, but worthwhile if you stick with it.

We are wise to ponder Peter's death, and destiny. He was not only one of the first disciples, but a leader among them, clearly in Jesus's inner circle. He followed Jesus into Jerusalem when he was arrested, hovering close by but not too close by. When asked by bystanders if he knew Jesus, he lied, and denied, not once but three times! How lovely then that, after Jesus was raised, on that day he cooked breakfast for the disciples by the sea, he took Peter aside and asked him—yes—three times "Do you love me?" Jesus, so wise, brought healing and reconciliation to his denier, forging bonds of love to root out the fear and guilt. No wonder Peter was the one who preached the first ever Christian sermon—on the day of Pentecost (Acts 2).

We might speak of Jesus's tomb being empty. Is Peter's empty? No. Some bones were found, and the tour displays them as perhaps the Church's most fantastic relic. Maybe Peter's. Maybe not. Either way, we all stay in our graves, our columbariums, our urns, or even the depths of the sea, awaiting the hope Peter staked everything on, and quite courageously, travelling to Rome to preach and be arrested, imprisoned, tried, and probably executed.

> *It's no longer what I want to do,*
> *or even what I want to do for God,*
> *but what God wants me to do.*

Jesus had said some haunting words to him after the three "Do you love me?" questions. "When you were young, you girded yourself and went wherever you wished. But when you grow old, you will stretch out your hands, and someone else will carry you where you do not wish to go" (John 21:18, my translation). And so it goes for all of us as we age, and so it goes for us when we say to the Lord, "Not my will, but your will be done." It's no longer what I want to do, or even what I want to do for God, but what God wants me to do.

# All Ye Citizens of Heaven

Visitors to Florence, Italy, love the Duomo, with its fantastic dome built by Brunelleschi in the 1420s—at the time the largest dome in the world, barely topping the Pantheon in Rome, which had been the largest for thirteen centuries! I love Ross King's book about how the dome came to be.[6] You can climb its 463 steps; I get short of breath just recalling it.

The church in Florence I love is Santa Croce. Just days after Lisa and I were there in 2017, a tile fell from the ceiling and killed a fifty-two year old tourist! There's so much to gawk at in this place, primarily (for someone with my tastes) the burials. In this one church, we have the tombs of Michelangelo, Galileo, Machiavelli (doesn't sound that holy, does he?), and Rossini. And there are monuments (at first I was fooled into thinking they, too, were buried there) to Leonardo da Vinci, Dante, the scientists Enrico Fermi and Guglielmo Marconi, and Florence Nightingale (though British, she was born in and named for the city).

I came, though, looking for St. Francis. He's buried in Assisi, of course, but the greatest artist devoted to showing us his life, Giotto, painted some astonishing frescoes right there in the Bardi Chapel of Santa Croce. Most tourists just glide right by, the chapel is so small, and seemingly insignificant next to the tombs of civilization's greatest heroes. But I love Giotto's work here, especially the scene of Francis having just died, his closest friends in grief and yet in praise of God. Lovely stuff.

Such paintings imprinted the eternal souls of such saints, like Francis, into the mindsets of those who came to church for worship, inspiration, comfort, and direction. I love the fact that, back in those days, the greats were buried right inside the church, not just outside in a cemetery, but actually under the floor, or in sarcophagi right on top of the floor. You see this in churches all over Europe. The saints are literally *in* the church, in the floors and walls, in the basements—reminding us that whenever we worship, we do so not merely with the people who actually show up that day, but with saints who've frequented the place over years and decades and, in the case of medieval cathedrals, centuries. We aren't alone. We have extraordinarily good company when we worship. At Christmas, we sing, "Sing, all ye citizens of heaven above."[7] Indeed. Due to the miracle the only God's amazing grace might provide for us, our predecessors in the Church and palpably if mystically and mysteriously present with us in the room, praising God, joining us in worship, and even urging us forward to higher depths of adoration and commitment to our God.

We are even one with people like Galileo and Machiavelli. So, first: Galileo. You may know the story, that this brilliant scientist, by looking closely at God's good creation, noticed that the earth isn't really the center of everything. It's not even the sun. We move about the sun, and the sun itself is in motion around something even larger, our galaxy—and even Galileo couldn't fathom all we know now about our universe and our place in it! He was called on the carpet by Church authorities for daring to suggest that the earth moves. He loved Jesus, and the Church, and so he stood before the stupid, irrationally rigid, yet powerful authorities and recanted—but then, according to the legend, as he exited the room he whispered, "But it does move," meaning the earth really does move around the sun.

I love this moment. The Church, getting things so very wrong, fearful of any slight change in thought, unable to catch up to how our faith might embrace the latest and truest knowledge that God-given and God-inspired humanity might discern, errs so terribly.

And then we find Machiavelli, his very name hitched to an adjective, *Machiavellian*, meaning "cunning, unscrupulous." How is he buried in such a great church? But then, how are any of us incorporated into God's extravagant work of grace and mercy that constitutes the historic convening of saints and sinners in the marvelous, surprising kingdom of God?

I am moved by theologian David Ford's lovely thought on Jesus's words that "In my father's house are many rooms" (or "mansions" as the King James Bible worded it): "'My Father's house' might be unimaginably capacious, and even those most at home there might meet many surprises—especially other people they do not expect, but also dimensions of truth and life."[8]

Could it be that, as I gaze on Machiavelli's tomb, so close to Michelangelo (who prized holiness above all else, and felt holiness was the key to his art), I realize how amazingly "capacious," roomy, spacious, and generous God's grace really is?

# The Incorruptibles

Let me add one more burial that fascinates me, this one with that whiff of the miraculous. We've mentioned St. Francis's friend and follower, St. Clare, who grew up in a house right up the street from Francis's family in Assisi. Movies have made her into his girlfriend. But she was much younger, and their only shared interest was their radical passion to serve Christ with total abandon. She formed a band of young women that paralleled the work of Francis and his friars.

When she died, they buried her temporarily in the San Giorgio church while a basilica (called Santa Chiara) in her memory was being built. That took seven years. When it was completed, they dug up her body and discovered that, without being embalmed or preserved in any way, it had not deteriorated. She is known still as one of the "Incorruptibles," saints who have died, with their bodies inexplicably never decomposing.[9] More than one hundred have been certified by the Catholic church, including St. Francis Xavier and St. Catherine of Genoa.

Easy to say Jesus's tomb is empty. I'm amazed, perplexed, and impressed by St. Clare and others: Their tombs are not empty; they're still there—as they were in life! Is this real? Faked somehow? That's what was asked about Jesus after Easter. And if it's a miracle, why would God bother? I asked this of my priest friend who first took me to the crypt of St. Clare's basilica to view her body behind glass. He said it's a sign, an occasional surprising clue to what is in store for the people of God, a little preview of the bodily resurrection to come.

I'm not sure what I (skeptic that I am) think. Yet I lean toward hoping and even kind of believing it's so. After all, if God could raise Jesus, and therefore if God could raise me and/or the people I love, why couldn't God preserve a human body to lure us into believing a little more than we might otherwise?

An incorruptible body or two might be more persuasive or at least palatable than some of what the church has attempted. One of the most fascinating displays of piety I've ever seen is a church in Rome not many people have heard about: *Santa Maria della Concezione dei Cappuccini*. In the crypt you can see the bones of 3,700 Capuchin friars arranged artistically into chapels, altars, and art depicting biblical scenes, crosses, and various saints. It's...creepy, macabre...although I can appreciate at the heart of it a valiant hope in the Resurrection. Those Capuchin brothers, all those monks, are dead—but already their bodily remains are functioning as an eternal church devoted to praising God.

# Where Death Happens

That cemetery in York where I laid my mother to rest on Ash Wednesday was a place she loved. In her retirement, she would load up her car with yard tools and spend a day a week raking, weeding, and scrubbing headstones. A little neighborhood of Marleys were nearby, and sometimes she told stories. One older brother was especially dear to her. She spoke of him as funny, a great musician, silly and tender, never dated or married. I could wonder what her generation didn't allow itself to wonder: Was he gay? Did he live his whole life as a secret?

The last time I drove my mother to visit the cemetery, since she was unable to weed or tidy things up, she knelt on her mama's grave, and then lay flat, facing down, arms spread as if reaching out to embrace her mama, who'd died so very young sixty-seven years earlier. She cried, spoke tenderly to her mama, and assured her she would be with her soon. I know there are those who avoid cemeteries, and I understand. I am one who wants, yea needs to visit, to sit a while, to have a talk, to say what might have been left unsaid. It's as if that Edicule, that little stone chapel around Jesus's now empty tomb, has opened up a branch establishment where those I've loved are, or aren't really anymore. I grieve. I hope. I commune.

But then, as much as I love to visit cemeteries—and we must see them on every trip we take as a family, beginning with our honeymoon in Hawaii!—I nod at the numbing truth Wendell Berry helped me understand in his marvelous novel *Jayber Crow*. Here's how he envisions Jayber reflecting on the death of his friend Forrest in World War II:

> I imagined that soldiers who are killed in war just disappear from the places where they are killed. Their deaths may be remembered by the comrades who saw them die, if the comrades live to remember. Their deaths will not be remembered where they happened. They will not be remembered in the halls of the government. Where do dead soldiers die who are killed in battle? They die at home—in Port William and thousands of other little darkened places, in thousands upon thousands of houses like Miss Gladdie's where The News comes, and everything on the tables and shelves is all of a sudden a relic and a reminder forever.[10]

Death happens in a hospital or out on a stretch of highway, and then the real death happens with family at home, and in the heart of God, and in the sacred places that are the church and loving memory. At the same time, our hope in the redemptive power of Jesus's death happens in all those places as well.

# Where I Didn't Want to Go

Speaking of a hospital. While I was in the early stages of writing this book, I had a sabbatical scheduled, with travel to Colorado and then Peru, then on to Israel and probably Iceland. But then I made an unanticipated journey to a place for which there are no guidebooks or fun photos on Facebook. I travelled just a mile from my home to the hospital—not as a professional visitor, but as a patient, admitted for the first time in my life. Instead of ministerial garb, there I was in the blousy green gown with a gaping opening in the back. Hard to discern whether to cling to your tattering shreds of dignity, or just surrender to no shame.

I mention this because we come face-to-face with death and resurrection most often in a hospital, even if we've been rushed there too late. My fifteen-day stay in the hospital began one evening with a suddenly fierce stomachache. I tried to tough it out. Lisa finally persuaded me to go to the ER. I expected a long wait, but within minutes a band of medical professionals were bustling around me with considerable urgency. A doctor said, "You need surgery." I asked, "When?" She said, "Right now." It was midnight, so I asked, "What if we wait?" She said, "You could die tonight."

I got my start in life in a hospital as a patient, sort of, if a baby in the nursery counts. And I knew before that surprising night that I may make my exit out of life in a hospital too. Such odd places, life and death, survival and decline mingled hauntingly in a single institution. I recall as a young pastor holding hands with an older gentleman as he breathed his last. Just as the nurse declared, "He's gone," the violins (was it Brahms?) on the loudspeaker announced a baby had just been born. *C'est la vie.*

In *Tuesdays with Morrie*, Mitch Albom tells of the day that his friend and teacher Morrie Schwartz was told he had Lou Gehrig's disease. "Outside, the sun was shining and people were going about their business. A woman ran to put money in the parking meter. Another carried groceries." Morrie was stunned by the normalcy of the day around him. *"Shouldn't the world stop? Don't they know what has happened to me?"*[11] Not that you want others to know. In our culture, which idolizes health, progress, and quick fixes, there's almost a sense of embarrassment that you haven't just whipped this thing. I was in the hospital way longer than anybody anticipated, and I could feel both concern but also shock that I wasn't home quickly. Tells us a lot about how good modern medicine is and about how we therefore blanch over the idea of extended suffering.

I've always loved hospital visitation, that holy chance to represent God's church to people under duress; I knew never to stay long (rule of thumb learned day one in seminary). As a patient in some misery, I found myself super honored someone would stop by. But I could muster zero hospitality energy, and I asked Lisa to hold folks at bay. I texted one visitor later to apologize for being rude. She understood. I hope. A couple of visitors just poked their heads in and waved. I felt so loved!—and relieved.

What to make of God and a long hospital stay? A lovely poem about illness by John O'Donohue speaks of "A courageous hospitality toward what is difficult, painful, and unknown."[12] On Day One, tethered to equipment and flat on a bed, I thought, "I'll pray a lot." It's embarrassingly difficult to pray when you're fending off constant nausea and a splitting headache, with various professionals zigging and zagging in and out to run tests, poke, stick, listen, prod. I veered quite a few times toward utter despair. I do know enough to recall that the Bible is full of despair. It's not something that mortifies Jesus. He is very close to us in our despair.

One of those professionals turned a light bulb on in my soul. A new nurse introduced himself: Martin. He asked how I was. This was at my nadir, the worst day and maybe hour ever. I said, "I'm despairing that I'm not getting better. I may never get better." He said, "You'll get better." I asked, "Is that a promise?" He laughed and said, "No, it's medicine."

Two things about that. We talk a lot about hope, or faith, as if it's something in us we have to do, and strongly if possible. But we hope in God, we believe in God. It's not our earnestness and positive thoughts about God, but God that saves us.

> *We talk a lot about hope, or faith, as if it's something in us we have to do, and strongly if possible. But we hope in God, we believe in God. It's not our earnestness and positive thoughts about God, but God that saves us.*

And then: medicine. We pray for cures. And God knows I might have prayed for more sick people in my lifetime than anyone you've ever met. God heals most often through the smart, hard-working, valiant professionals we call doctors, nurses, the IV team, the X-ray and CT scan people who are God's handymen, delegates, worker bees, elves . . . so don't go as far as you can go with medicine and then ask God to overcome what they can't fix. God is already there when, after your physical, the internist orders up an extra test. God is even in you, God's delegate, in your body, the Temple of the Holy Spirit: When you feel pain or discomfort (as I did to start all this), it's God saying "James! James! I wired you with these warning signals! Go see my people down there who can help!"

I have a friend who heard I was laid low, and said "God sure has a way of slowing you down." I can't think for a moment God thought, "James is just wearing himself out being so busy! I'll jerk this colonic volvulus thing in his gut, and then he'll cool his jets for a while." But there is a simplification, a cutting to the core of what really matters. O'Donohue's poem suggests illness might become "a lantern to illuminate new qualities that will emerge in you," and that this light might "release whatever has become false in you."[13] Once it became evident I'd be in the hospital for quite a few days, and I'd emerge sub-par whenever I got out, I cancelled a week of busy things to do in about ten minutes. Important and urgent, some of these things! But all tumbled rapidly off the table of what really matters, as did trips to Colorado and Peru planned for my sabbatical. Funny how little they mattered in the face of a health crisis!

For me, and I pray I can cling to this more zealously than I clung to my last shred of dignity being prodded in that green gown, it's understanding what really matters—that is, what it is to be human. To be human isn't to make mistakes. To be human isn't to consume or maximize fun. My fellow human temporary boarders in the hospital? Not one of us wanted to be there. Yet every one of us very much wanted to be there. Like life on earth, it's a pilgrimage, we're passing through—but gosh, it's such a cool space. And it took me a week to realize I didn't know the political or religious affiliation of any other patient or professional. Lovely. Calming. Healing.

We are alive in these bodies. It's precarious, always—which is what makes it such a treasure. I'm here. My wife and kids are hovering nearby. Life is good. Life is hard. Life is…life. I'm a person who matters, if only in this small space to not many people.

Which is why I made it a point to ask every professional her or his name, and where are you from? No one responded with merely a city or state. Always a story. So many stories: people with jobs, but dreamers, lovers, with their own issues and gifts and glories. I might just wear this hospital wristband forever to remind me of just that. Being human. That's all God asks of us. That's all God asks us to ask of one another.

# NOTES

## Introduction: Everywhere Is the Holy Land

1   Madeleine L'Engle, "The Risk of Birth, Christmas, 1973," *The Ordering of Love* (Colorado Springs, Colorado: WaterBrook, 2005), 155.

2   Regis J. Armstrong, J.A. Wayne Hellmann, William J. Short, eds., *Francis of Assisi: Early Documents*, vol. I (Hyde Park, New York: New City Press, 2002), 255.

3   Matthew Fox, *Passion for Creation: The Earth-Honoring Spirituality of Meister Eckhart* (Rochester, Vermont: Inner Traditions, 2000), 336.

## Chapter 1. Everywhere Is Galilee: The Downward Call

1   Maggie Ross, *The Fountain & the Furnace: The Way of Tears and Fire* (New York: Paulist Press, 1987), 80.

2   Cited and discussed in my *Conversations with St. Francis* (Nashville: Abingdon Press, 2008), 2ff.

3   *Francis of Assisi: Early Documents*, vol. 2, ed. Regis J. Armstrong, J. A. Wayne Hellman, William J. Short (New York: New City Press, 2000), 251.

4   *Mother Maria Skobtsova: Essential Writings*, ed. Helene Klepinin-Arjokovsky (Maryknoll, New York: Orbis, 2003), 115.

5   Eddie S. Glaude Jr., *Begin Again: James Baldwin's America and Its Urgent Lessons for Our Own* (New York: Crown, 2020), 31.

6   Taylor Branch, *Parting the Waters: America in the King Years 1954-63* (New York: Simon and Schuster, 1988), 166-67.

7   Branch, *Parting the Waters*, 149.

8   Henri Nouwen, *¡Gracias!: A Latin American Journal* (San Francisco: Harper & Row, 1983), 11.

9   Robert Robinson, "Come Thou Fount of Every Blessing," *The United Methodist Hymnal* (Nashville: The United Methodist Publishing House, 1989), 400, stanza 3.

# Notes

10   William E. Wallace, *Michelangelo, God's Architect* (Princeton: Princeton University, 2019), 9.

11   Wallace, *Michelangelo*, 9.

## Chapter 2. Everywhere Is the Jordan: Baptism and All the Waters

1   Norman Maclean, *A River Runs Through It: and Other Stories* (Chicago: University of Chicago Press, 2017), 119.

2   Edward Achorn, *The Lincoln Miracle: Inside the Republican Convention That Changed History* (New York: Atlantic Monthly Press, 2023), 160.

3   Paul Elie, *Reinventing Bach* (New York: Farrar Straus and Giroux, 2013), 409.

4   Reynolds Price, *A Whole New Life: An Illness and a Healing* (New York: Scribner, 1982), 43.

5   Rowan Williams, *Being Christian: Baptism, Bible, Eucharist, Prayer* (Grand Rapids: Wm. B. Eerdmans, 2014), 10.

6   Reinhold Niebuhr, *The Irony of American History* (New York: Charles Scribner's Sons, 1952), 63.

7   Linnie Marsh Wolfe, *Son of the Wilderness: The Life of John Muir* (Madison, Wisconsin: University of Wisconsin Press, 1945), 144.

## Chapter 3. Everywhere Is the Mount of Olives: Standing Up and Courage

1   William H. Parker, "Tell Me the Stories of Jesus," *The United Methodist Hymnal* (Nashville: The United Methodist Publishing House, 1989), 277, stanza 3.

2   Roland Bainton, *Here I Stand: The Life of Martin Luther* (New York: Abingdon, 1950), 183-5.

3   Glaude, *Begin Again*, 31.

4   "Demonstrators in Selma Mark 30th Anniversary of March Across Edmund Pettus Bridge," *Jet*, March 27, 1995, 24.

5   David Halberstam, *The Children* (New York: Fawcett, 1998), 140.

6   Jon Meacham, *His Truth is Marching On: John Lewis and the Power of Hope* (New York: Random House, 2020), 248.

7   References in my *Conversations with St. Francis*, 93f. I am proud that this episode, not well known, is enshrined in stained glass in the Davidson United Methodist Church sanctuary, which was built during my tenure.

8   Barnette, *Clarence Jordan*, 33.

9   Dietrich Bonhoeffer, *Letters and Papers from Prison*, ed. Eberhard Bethge (New York: Macmillan, 1971), p. 77. The following quotations are from pages 271, 17, 234, 10, 361, and 11.

10  Eberhard Bethge, *Dietrich Bonhoeffer: Man of Vision, Man of Courage*, tr. Edwin Robertson (London: Collins, 1970), 831.

11  Marilynne Robinson, *Gilead* (New York: Farrar, Straus, Giroux, 2004), 246.

12  *English Omnibus of the Sources for the Life of St. Francis*, ed. Marion Habig (Chicago: Franciscan Herald, 1973), 1448.

## Chapter 4. Everywhere Is Bethlehem: Prayer Walls

1  Sue Monk Kidd, *The Secret Life of Bees* (New York: Penguin, 2003), 96.

2  Jonathan Eig, *King: A Life* (New York: Farrar, Straus and Giroux, 2023), 156-8.

3  Augustine, *Confessions*, 3:21, translated by Sarah Ruden (New York: Modern Library, 2017), 74.

4  Mary Oliver, *Felicity* (New York: Penguin, 2016), 3.

5  *Confessions*, 9.29, p. 268-69.

6  Julian of Norwich, *Revelations of Divine Love* (Garden City, New York: Image, 1977), 107, 124

7  Ken Follett, *Notre-Dame: A Short History of the Meaning of Cathedrals* (New York: Viking, 2019), 3.

8  Ken Follett, The *Pillars of the Earth* (New York: Penguin, 1989), 18.

9  Jan Milič Lochman, *The Lord's Prayer*, ed. Daniel Migliore (Grand Rapids: Wm. B. Eerdmans, 1993), 18.

10  Simon Jenkins, *Cathedrals: Masterpieces of Architecture, Feats of Engineering, Icons of Faith* (New York: Rizzoli, 2021), 24.

11  Philip Williamson, "Churchill and the Churches," *Finest Hour*, January 1,1970, 12. Accessed October 12, 2023. https://winstonchurchill.org /publications/finest-hour/finest-hour-191/churchill-and-the-churches/.

12  Robert Barron, *Heaven in Stone and Glass: Experiencing the Spirituality of the Great Cathedrals* (New York: Crossroad, 2000), 11.

13  Barron, *Heaven in Stone and Glass*, 13.

14  Barron, *Heaven in Stone and Glass*, 97.

15  Barron, *Heaven in Stone and Glass*, 48.

16  Magnus Magnusson, *Lindisfarne: The Cradle Island* (Stroud: The History Press, 1984), 52.

## Chapter 5. Everywhere Is Nazareth: Finding the Way Home

1  With unmatched eloquence, Sam Wells ruminates on this season and the cruciality of God being "with" us in *A Nazareth Manifesto: Being with God* (Chichester, West Sussex. United Kingdom: John Wiley & Sons, 2015).

2  Augustine, *Confessions*, I.1.

# Notes

3     Jad Abumrad, "Tennessee Mountain Trance," October 29, 2019, in Dolly Parton's America, produced by Shima Oliaee, podcast, MP3 audio, 41:21, https://www.wnycstudios.org/podcasts/dolly-partons-america/episodes /tennessee-mountain-trance.

4     Robinson, *Gilead*, 57.

5     Jim Forest, *Love Is the Measure: a Biography of Dorothy Day* (Maryknoll: Orbis, 1994), 135.

6     Ellen F. Davis, *Preaching the Luminous Word* (Grand Rapids: Eerdmans, 2016), 2.

7     Isabel Wilkerson, *Caste* (New York: Random House, 2020), 13.

8     Jonathan Sacks, *Studies in Spirituality* (Jerusalem: Maggid, 2021), 15.

9     Chris Matthews, *Hardball* (New York: Simon and Schuster, 1999), 229.

10    Thomas Merton, *Thoughts in Solitude* (New York: Farrar, Straus & Giroux, 1956), 99.

**Chapter 6. Everywhere Is Jerusalem: Places of Sorrow and Hope**

1     Pat Conroy, *The Prince of Tides* (New York: Bantam, 1987), 310f.

2     Greg Melville, *Over My Dead Body: Unearthing the Hidden History of America's Cemeteries* (New York: Henry N. Abrams, 2022), 97.

3     The Genocide Education Project, "Hitler and the Armenian Genocide," Accessed October 16, 2023, https://genocideeducation.org/background /hitler-and-the-armenian-genocide/.

4     Glaude, *Begin Again*, 186.

5     Barbara Kingsolver, *Animal Dreams* (New York: Harper Perennial, 1990), 168.

6     Ross King, *Brunelleschi's Dome* (New York: Bloomsbury, 2013), 161.

7     John Wade, "O Come, All Ye Faithful," *The United Methodist Hymnal* (Nashville: The United Methodist Publishing House, 1989), 234, stanza 3.

8     David F. Ford, *The Gospel of John* (Grand Rapids: Baker, 2021), 272.

9     Joan Carroll Cruz, *The Incorruptibles: A Study of the Incorruption of the Bodies of Various Catholic Saints and Beati* (Charlotte: TAN, 1977).

10    Wendell Berry, *Jayber Crow* (Berkeley: Counterpoint, 2000), 141.

11    Mitch Albom, *Tuesdays with Morrie* (New York: Penguin, 1997), 8.

12    John O'Donohue, *To Bless the Space Between Us* (New York: Doubleday, 2008), 60.

13    O'Donohue, *To Bless the Space Between Us*, 61.

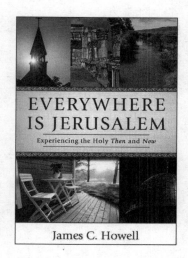